I gotta KNow!

Al Denson

WITH PAT SPRINGLE

TYNDALE HOUSE PUBLISHERS, INC.
WHEATON, ILLINOIS

Library of Congress Cataloging-in-Publication Data

Denson, Al.
    I gotta know! / Al Denson with Pat Springle.
        p.   cm.
    Includes bibliographical references.
    ISBN 0-8423-3859-4 (pbk. : alk. paper)
    1. Teenagers—Religious life. 2. Teenagers—Conduct of life.
I. Springle, Pat, date. II. Title.
BV4531.2.D465 1999
248.8'3—dc21   98-48045

Printed in the United States of America

05 04 03 02 01 00 99
7   6   5   4   3   2   1

I dedicate this book
to all youth pastors
who work day in and
day out to change the lives of young people
in their communities. May God continue to renew
your excitement about helping to change today's youth.
I pray that this book helps you
deal with those tough times of ministry.

MisSioN StATemeNT

TO BE a creatively driven artist that will lead the Christian music industry by providing the public with an excellent message of Christ through the talents God has given me.

TO ALWAYS LIVE the words I write in my everyday life through the actions I take and the words I speak.

TO MAINTAIN a high level of integrity in my dealing with people and always strive for excellence in everything I do, as it is an expectation of myself and not just a goal.

Al Denson
Celebration Ministries

CoNTentS

Section 4: Love and Sex

Section 5: Friends and School

Section 6: Family Problems

Section 7: Questions about My Sanity

Conclusion

FoREword

AL DENSON is the real deal. His love is real, his genuine interest in teens and their future is real, and his God-given musical ability is effective beyond human explanation.

I so much believe in the effectiveness of Al Denson that we at LIFE Outreach International and *LIFE Today* (our daily television program) have wholeheartedly embraced, endorsed, and supported his efforts. We do this both prayerfully and financially and will continue to do so.

Because I spent more than twenty years of my life leading high school assemblies and various youth outreaches, I know what it takes to reach youth. Al Denson has unlimited potential in youth ministry. He communicates powerfully! He generates enthusiasm in positive directions and inspires change that can be brought about only by supernatural enabling.

When Al exalts Jesus as the one way to the Father, to true character, and to meaningful life, kids respond with their whole heart. The result is immediate change in desire and direction. He presents what the youth of America are crying out for: someone to care, someone to lead, someone to give real answers that last for eternity.

The questions kids are asking and the life-transforming answers presented in this book are must-reading for the youth of North America and for those who care about kids. Join Al in getting the truth out!

James Robison
President and Founder
LIFE Outreach International

Let me begin my many thanks by recognizing the one reason I am who I am—Jesus Christ. Because of him and his unconditional grace and love, I have the ability to bring his truth to others.

To my wife, Tracie: I could never thank you enough for all the sacrifices you've made to support me. It amazes me that you know me so well and love me anyway!

Pat Springle is a very wise man. Thank you for the valuable input throughout some of the tough questions.

My board of directors (especially Don Sapaugh and Wes Christian) has contributed so much to my life and the life of Celebration Ministries. Thank you for the many hours of support, guidance, and ever-needed wisdom; without all of this I just might go crazy!

I would also like to thank the following people: Mom and Dad, Rich, Denny, BJ, Amanda, and David Denson, Celebration staff, Jeff Calhoun, Dawson McAllister, Paul and Deanna Reardon, Ed Young Jr. (my pastor), James Robison, John Morgan (my other pastor), George and Linda Gleason, Charlie Sharp, Denton Goode, Jay Strack, Ron Hutchcraft, Lifeline, Martin Coleman, Trish Ragsdale, FamNet, Benson Records, Ambassador Agency, and the incredible Tyndale House Publishers.

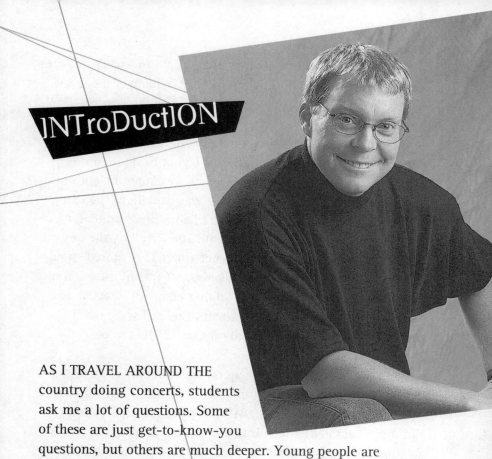

INTroDuctION

AS I TRAVEL AROUND THE
country doing concerts, students
ask me a lot of questions. Some
of these are just get-to-know-you
questions, but others are much deeper. Young people are
searching. They want answers—real answers—from people who
really care about them.

I've seen teenagers whose questions were answered. They
walked away with a sense of hope that now they would know
how to respond to the pressures they face. They may not have
grasped every detail of their problem or the solution, but at
least they felt understood and had a new sense of confidence
that God would help them work it out.

But I've also seen those whose questions weren't answered.
Maybe I didn't understand their questions. Or maybe I didn't
take enough time to listen so I could get beneath the surface

and hear the *real* questions they were afraid to ask. Or maybe I gave answers they didn't want to hear. Whatever the cause, it hurts to see young people struggle. I know how it feels. I've been there myself.

When I was in high school, I really wanted to be accepted. I stayed up late at night all the time trying to figure out how to get people to like me. When I was a freshman, I went out for football . . . because my brother was captain of the team, and jocks were cool and respected. I had a small problem: I was only four feet eight inches tall. The first day, the guys on the team stuffed me in the locker where they stored shoulder pads. They locked it and walked out. I was in there a long time! But I didn't yell at them. I didn't complain. I acted as if I liked it . . . because I wanted them to think I was cool. I stayed in that locker with smelly jockstraps just to be accepted.

The next day, they put me up on the rafters in the ceiling. The coach came in and saw my feet dangling in the air. One of the guys whispered, "Hey, Al! Lift your feet up!" When I did, I accidentally banged into the ceiling. Some ceiling tiles fell, and I fell with them! I landed on the floor in that pile of broken tiles, and all the guys laughed their heads off! Some people might have felt embarrassed if that had happened to them, but I felt so cool being the center of attention. I felt accepted.

Another time I locked myself in a tuba case to see if my friends in the band would put me on the bus. They did, and I thought I was the coolest guy around.

That's how I tried to be accepted. I got attention. That's what I wanted.

You may be a *student* who's reading this book because you want to find out what other students are thinking and feeling.

That's great! You may have some specific questions you've wanted to ask somebody . . . but you were afraid to speak up. I hope you find what you're looking for in these pages.

You may be a *friend* of a student who is struggling, and you want to help your friend. That's great! Your care and concern for your friend is worth more than you can imagine. Be careful, though, that you don't smother the person with attention and advice. Being a friend doesn't mean controlling the other person's behavior. It means listening and caring, sharing your own experience, and only sparingly giving advice.

You may be a *parent* who wants to understand your teenager better. Maybe you've given some advice in the past and, well, let's just say it wasn't received very well! Sometimes young people don't want advice. They may need it desperately, but they won't listen unless we communicate on their terms. I hope this book helps you do that.

You may be a *youth group leader* who's looking for specific answers to specific questions. Use this as a reference book. You may want to let the students in your ministry read the answers themselves. Or you can use the book as a launching pad that will take teens to the Scriptures as you explain how God has used the truths in your own life.

Whether you are an adolescent or a person like me who cares about adolescents, be sure to read the conclusion that follows the questions and answers. You'll find additional suggestions for getting help and for learning to interact with others in positive ways.

Al Denson

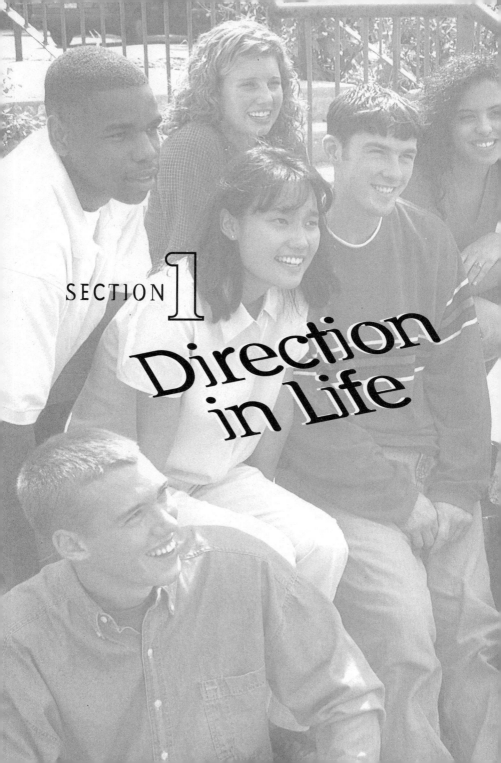

SECTION 1

Direction in Life

Hope for the American Student

When you feel as if nobody cares and you need someone to talk to, call the HOPELINE: 1-800-394-4673.

A caring encourager will be on the line to offer you hope from a biblical perspective 24 hours a day, 7 days a week, 365 days a year.

"Every adult fully aware . . . every student receiving care!"

1
What should be the top priorities in my life?

AT 3:40 IN THE AFTERNOON on December 18, 1994, God took hold of my priorities. At that moment, the small plane in which I was flying with two friends crashed. The friend sitting next to me died. My face was cut up into a zillion pieces, and it took months for me to get going again. I sure don't know all the reasons why God allowed that plane to crash, but I know one thing: It made me stop and take a long look at my life. I was going too fast, doing too much. In the months after the crash, God brought balance back into my life. Balance is a hard thing to find. Sometimes God whispers to get our attention. If we don't hear him, he speaks a little louder. That plane crash was God's voice in a sonic boom!

Deciding what is really important—and sticking with those choices no matter what—is one of the hardest things we will do in life. (At least it is in my life!) It's fairly easy to separate the bad from the good. It's a lot harder to find the *best* among all the good things!

As busy as your life is now, it will get only more complicated later. Now is the time to figure out what's important. Talk to God, read the Scriptures, and talk to your youth pastor about the things that really matter. Ask yourself the questions: What does God want for me? What are *his* priorities for my life? And here's a really hard one: *Am I willing to do whatever God wants me to do?*

Write down your priorities. Then look at the sheet long and hard. Maybe you're like me: Writing things down makes me a lot more serious about them; somehow, seeing them in black and white makes them a lot clearer. You might just find that some of your priorities need to change. (And some of them may need to be chucked!) Writing and reflecting will sharpen your priorities and make them line up more with what God wants for your life.

As you determine what's really important, you can set your priorities. Then you can make a specific plan of action each day. Someone once said, "Plan your day or someone else will plan it for you." Teenagers need time to hang out with each other, but many of them have no priorities and no plan at all . . . except to kill time with their friends! Find something that turns your crank! That will make it much easier to channel your energies into productive activities. Then you can schedule how you use your time, but you can still be open to any interruptions God may bring your way.

As I've tried to walk with God, these are the priorities I've learned are most important:

1. Developing my relationship with Christ. I try to spend time with him on a daily basis by talking to him and listening to his Word. I carve out time (and that's hard!) to read, study, and memorize the Scriptures. I try to get to *know* God, not just know *about* him.

A man asked Jesus, "Teacher, which is the most important commandment in the law of Moses?" (Matthew 22:36). There are hundreds of commands in the Old Testament, but Jesus quickly pointed to one above all the others. He told the man, "You must love the Lord your God with all your heart, all your soul, and all your mind" (Matthew 22:37). Knowing and loving God is the most important thing in my life, your life, and anybody else's life—whether we know it or not!

As we are drawing strength and insight from Christ, something terrific happens to us: His love and power flow out of our life, and we are able to have a powerful impact on others. Jesus compared this flow to an unstoppable river: "On the last day, the climax of the festival, Jesus stood and shouted to the crowds, 'If you are thirsty, come to me! If you believe in me, come and drink! For the Scriptures declare that rivers of living water will flow out from within'" (John 7:37-38). An overflow of God's love—that's what he was talking about! And that's what happens when we "drink" Christ's grace and strength.

But don't we need food and clothes, sports and friends? You bet! However, we need to see these things as *gifts from God*. Jesus' disciples wondered about this. So Jesus told them, "Your heavenly Father . . . will give you all you need from day to day if you live for him and make the Kingdom of God your primary concern" (Matthew 6:32-33).

Maybe it goes without saying, but I'm going to say it anyway: Our relationship with Christ is "rooted and grounded" in the truths of Scripture. There are a lot of harebrained ideas out there about God! Study the Bible to see what's true and what's baloney. Now I'm not going to tell you that every book of the Bible is stimulating and easy to read. Some parts are pretty difficult. Focus on the parts that are clear and meaningful. (I like Matthew, Mark, Luke, and John; I also like Paul's letters, such as Ephesians and Philippians.) Maybe later (much later!) you can memorize Deuteronomy!

2. Loving people. Do you remember the passage in which the man asked Jesus what was the most important commandment? Jesus didn't stop after he said the number one priority is to love God with all your heart. He then said, "A second [commandment] is equally important: 'Love your neighbor as yourself'" (Matthew 22:39). Loving people is the natural (maybe I should say *super*natural!) result of experiencing God's love. The apostle John wrote, "God . . . sent his Son as a sacrifice to take away our sins. Dear friends, since God loved us that much, we surely ought to love each other" (1 John 4:10-11).

And who is the "neighbor" Jesus tells us to love?

- *Family.* This is an easy one for me! But it may not be that easy for other people because not all families are refuges from the storms of life. In fact, some families *create* the storms of life!
- *Other believers.* Some Christians are easy to love, aren't they? But I know a few. . . . Still, if we are drinking deeply of the love of Christ, we'll be able to channel that love toward people who are hard to love.
- *Unbelievers.* And some unbelievers are easy to be around. (In fact, some are a lot easier to hang around than some of the grumpy Christians I know!) But there are some obnoxious people who seem to want to test every bit of faith we have. Some of them may even be . . .

- *Enemies.* One of the hardest things to do is to love people who set themselves against us, lie about us, and make fun of us. But Jesus and Paul instruct us to love our enemies (see Matthew 5:44 and Romans 12:14). *You can tell how much you love God by how much you love the person you like the least!*

As we walk with Christ and feast on his Word, other priorities will have their proper place, including:

3. Attending church. The church is the bride of Christ. She is the one he died for and is coming back for. Don't underestimate the importance of the church. If you are going to have a growing relationship with the Lord, you need to worship, fellowship, serve, and be taught in relationship to others in the family of God. Only the church can meet these needs.

4. Doing my best at school or on the job. For now, school occupies your time. Later, when your education is complete, a job will take its place. Going to school and doing well in a job are important. Work hard and do the best you can, making the most of every opportunity that comes your way.

5. Taking time for recreation. This is a no-brainer for a lot of young people, but some are so focused on school or work that they need some help to learn to enjoy their friends, hobbies, sports, or whatever helps them relax and stay healthy. This includes social, mental, physical, and emotional health.

A word of advice: Don't kill yourself trying to do everything. The Bible tells us to be moderate in most things in life, except for one thing—our love for Jesus Christ. God wants us to be absolutely sold out, radical, and 100 percent committed to him. As you spend time in God's Word and around mature, godly people, you will learn to be balanced in the other areas of your life.

Remembering this might help:

These are the priorities I've learned are most important: (1) developing my relationship with Christ; (2) loving people—the supernatural result of experiencing God's love; (3) attending church; (4) doing my best at school or on the job; (5) taking time for recreation.

2

I want a lot of stuff. Is there anything wrong with that?

WHEN I WAS NINE YEARS OLD, a neighbor's house burned down just before Christmas. The family lost everything. Mom and Dad decided we would each pick out a gift from under our tree to give to that family. My two brothers and I eyeballed all the presents under our tree. I don't know if you're like me, but I can tell what's in every box even when it's wrapped. I knew which present was the one I really, really wanted, and I knew which ones were underwear and socks. I picked up one of the boxes I didn't care about. Out of the corner of my eye, I saw my mom looking at me. She had *that* look on her face, which said, "Are you *sure* you picked up the one you want to give?" I put the box down and picked up the one with the gift I really wanted.

We went over to see that family. I remember watching the kid open the gift I brought, and I can still see the look on his face. It was the coolest computer game I'd ever seen. He was so excited! At that second, it all made sense. I realized I didn't really care about things. I did really care about helping other people.

A friend of mine has a poster on his wall. It says, "Happiness is wanting what you have, not having what you want." There's a ton of wisdom in that statement!

First, you need to understand that there is nothing wrong

with having material things. God says in 1 Timothy 6:17 that he "richly gives us all we need for our enjoyment." But the first part of that verse is a warning. It says, "Tell those who are rich in this world not to be proud and not to trust in their money, which will soon be gone. But their trust should be in the living God." If we see clothes, cars, sports duds, and trips as gifts from God, these things will take the right place in our heart. Otherwise, they become idols, taking the place of God in our affections and desires.

If you are preoccupied with having more and finer things, you need to ask yourself why material things are so important to you.

- Maybe you compare yourself to others at school who have better stuff than you have. The "rich kids" may seem to be a little more popular, and this is the conclusion you might draw: "If I had nicer stuff, I'd be more popular too!"
- Maybe you feel empty, and you think happiness is just another purchase away.
- Maybe you don't feel very good about yourself, and you think having the right clothes or the latest "toy" will impress people and make them like you.
- Maybe buying things is a way to comfort yourself.
- Maybe you demand material things as a substitute for your parents' love. If your parents don't provide what you need, you may become angry and make unreasonable demands on your parents for material things. What you really want, though, is your parents' time, attention, and love.

If any statement above is true for you, possessions own you—you don't own them!

As we walk with Christ, we will learn to see possessions as gifts. Then we can live with 'em or without 'em. We'll be free to let material things take their rightful place in our life. We won't give in to all the advertisements we're bombarded with every day.

Practically every commercial on television, every ad on the radio, and every billboard along the highway communicates the message "If you only had our product or service, you'd be happier!" (Hey, check them out and see if I'm wrong!) Beer commercials promise that if you slurp their suds, you'll have gorgeous babes and buff boys laughing and playing ball with you. Sure, some people laugh together when they drink beer, but what about all the heartache created by booze? Toothpaste commercials promise that their brand will win you the date of your dreams. But as long as you brush your buckies, who cares what toothpaste you use? Jeans commercials promise they can make you look like a million dollars . . . for only thirty-five dollars! Actually, jeans are just some heavy fabric sewn together. *Things* aren't the source of true happiness, are they? No, I don't think so!

The problem is that we have believed so many of the advertisers' promises that we don't even think anymore! Everywhere we go we're flooded by the constant appeals to buy, buy, buy, and each commercial has to promise a little more than the one before. We need to wise up! One of the things I like to do is to ask myself and my family, "What is the promise in this commercial? What does it say— or at least imply—that I'll get if I buy that product?" To tell you the truth, this gets us a lot of laughs! We howl at the absurdities! Why don't you try it too?

OK, that's fun to do, but let me get serious for a minute. Envy—wanting things other people have—will eat your spiritual lunch! It will eat away at your heart and consume it. Don't let your love for Christ be destroyed by the petty desire to have more things, bigger things, and newer things. The fact is that people who have lots of stuff really aren't any happier. Oh, they may get a rush for a day or two after they get something, but the feeling doesn't last. And many of them think about getting more and more stuff day after day. Obsessing about buying stuff sure doesn't build good, deep relationships! God made us so that only he can fill up the hole in our heart. Things never can.

Remembering this might help:

Happiness is wanting what you have, not having what you want.

3

How can I handle money wisely . . . and not blow it all?

MY MOM AND DAD USED TO MAKE my brothers and me give to the church 10 percent of any money we earned. We could do whatever we wanted with the rest of it. I kept my money in a big glass jar in my room at home. At one point, our church was trying to raise money for a new building. My pastor, Brother John, brought some cattle troughs (big metal bowls cows drink from) to the front of the church. He asked people to bring the best they had for the church building and put it in the troughs. I was sitting in the choir that morning, and the Lord tapped me on the shoulder. I got up while Brother John was speaking, and I ran home to get my jar of money. I was only fourteen, so I didn't have my driver's license. That's why I had to run.

I got back to the church, went over to the keyboard, and played while the choir sang. We didn't have any pews yet, and the stage was just concrete. No heat, just some droplights. No carpet, just concrete floors. When Brother John called for people to come forward so they could put their gifts to God in the cattle troughs, people brought rifles, wedding rings, and all kinds of valuable stuff for the church to sell. I took my money jar up and put it in. That day taught me a lot about handling money. To be a good steward of money, I needed to be willing to give it all away at any time.

The ability to manage money is a mark of real maturity. That ability is determined by how responsible a person is. To tell you the truth, I know some teenagers who are very good at this, and I know some adults who are horrible at it! (In fact, one of the main reasons for trouble in marriage relationships is that at least one of the partners is irresponsible about money.)

Paul was very clear when he wrote to Timothy regarding money: "For the love of money is at the root of all kinds of evil. And some people, craving money, have wandered from the faith and pierced themselves with many sorrows" (1 Timothy 6:10). Notice that Paul didn't say *money* is evil. He said "the *love* of money is at the root of all kinds of evil." Money itself is neutral. How we *use* money is good or evil.

Did you know that Jesus had more to say about money than about almost any other subject? He talked about it even more than heaven or hell. He warned people against letting the pursuit of money control their life. He said, "No one can serve two masters. For you will hate one and love the other, or be devoted to one and despise the other. You cannot serve both God and money" (Matthew 6:24).

You might hear this and think, *Serve money? What is Jesus talking about?* Good questions! It is a question of lordship: Are we actively pursuing the kingdom of God, or do we spend our time and energies on getting money and things?

One of the biggest problems in our society today—even among Christians—is debt. We get things, but they don't really satisfy us, and we want "a little more." That "little more" is a bit beyond our ability to pay, so we borrow money to get it. (Banks are issuing credit cards to high school students these days, in case you didn't know that.) A person may have every intention of being satisfied with the thing he bought, and he may plan to pay it off. But a funny thing happens—he wants something else, too! So he borrows to buy that. And again. And again. And again. Pretty soon, the person is so far in debt that he spends his whole life trying to earn enough money just to pay the interest each month! Now that's slavery!

OK, you may not have a credit card and be up to your eyeballs in debt. Good for you! All you want to know is how to get enough money to buy that good-looking shirt you saw at the mall and have enough left over to go to the concert this weekend. All right, get ready. I'm going to talk about the *b* word. That's right. *Budget!* No matter how much or how little money a person has, he needs to operate on a budget or he can get into *big* trouble! I don't really like having a budget for our family or for my ministry, but I have to have one. Too much is riding on my being responsible to handle finances wisely for me to spend whatever I want, hoping there'll be enough to cover all the expenses.

Some teenagers get an allowance from their parents; some just ask for money whenever they need it. I strongly encourage you to learn good money management by having a fixed allowance that forces you to make decisions about how to spend it. After a while (certainly after you finish college, but even in high school for many people), you will earn your own money and not be dependent on your parents. A summer job while you're in high school and college will help you understand the value of hard-earned dollars.

You don't have to have a spreadsheet and the latest Windows software to establish and stay on a budget! All you need is two columns—income and expenses. For each period of time (weekly or monthly), determine how much money you will have and how you plan to spend it. For instance, expenses might include clothes, movies, concerts, sports events, dates, gas and oil for your car (even your parents' car!), thirty-seven bottles of fingernail polish (for the ladies), tank tops to show off your pecs (for the guys), and of course, mad money!

As you budget, don't forget where the money comes from. Whether parents give you an allowance or you earn the money yourself, you need to give some back to God on a regular basis. You should give out of appreciation because "God loves the person who gives cheerfully" (2 Corinthians 9:7).

One more thing: Put a little money aside each week or month in savings. You might want to open a savings account, or you might want to keep the money in a jar on a shelf—unless you have a little brother or sister with sticky fingers! And if you save enough, you might want to invest some money. Even high school students can learn about all the investment options. You can buy some shares of stock and watch the value grow—hopefully! Even if you don't open a savings account or invest the money, you can keep some stashed away for emergency expenses . . . like a new pair of tennis shoes that cost more than the gross national product of Bolivia!

Staying on a budget might be pretty hard at first, but you'll get the hang of it. Learn now to be responsible with money. You'll be really glad later in life. (Your spouse and children will be glad too!)

John Wesley was a great leader of a spiritual awakening in America and England in the early eighteenth century. He was the founder of the Methodist church. Wesley said this about money: "Earn all you can. Save all you can. And give all you can." That's good advice for all of us. If we're responsible, we'll earn what we need to live on, save for future needs or emergencies, and give away as much as we can to those in need.

Ultimately, the way we handle money is a demonstration of our heart's desires and direction. Learn to handle money in a way that honors the Lord!

Remembering this might help:

Earn all you can. Save all you can. And give all you can.

4

How can I find God's will for my life?

LIFE CAN GET PRETTY CONFUSING SOMETIMES . . .
especially when you are trying to define your own identity.
At certain points, it's really hard to know what to do. One
of the things that encourages me in those times is the assurance that God has a plan for my life. When things were at
their worst for the children of Israel, Jeremiah spoke God's
words to them: "'For I know the plans I have for you,' says
the Lord. 'They are plans for good and not for disaster, to
give you a future and a hope'" (Jeremiah 29:11).

Just as God created each person to be a unique individual,
he has a unique plan for each of us. Satan has done a good
job of convincing some Christians that God's will for them is
something awful—like marrying an ugly person or living
in a desert or eating bugs for a lifetime! Because of the devil's
deception, we treat God's will like an invitation to a nerd
party!

God's will is great! His will is what is best for us. If we find
it and do it, we'll have God's best. He really will give us a
wonderful, abundant life.

God isn't trying to hide his will from us. In fact, he wants
you to know it more than you do. He wants to give you
direction for right decisions, like which college to attend,
whom to marry, or what to do with your life.

God's will begins for you the moment you become a Christian. From that moment, you can expect God to continually reveal his will to you.

When there is a problem in discovering God's will, it lies with us, not him. Christians usually fall into one of three groups concerning God's will:

1. Those who really don't want to know God's will.
2. Those who want to know his will but agree to follow it only if they like what they hear.
3. Those who want to know God's will and are willing to say yes even before they know what it is.

Here is a good question to ask yourself: "What is my attitude toward God's will?" That is an important question for all of us! Perhaps you fit into one of the first two groups above. If so, how about praying to become part of the third group?

God's plan for each of us is always in keeping with these basic principles:

- God wants us to love him with all our heart and, in response to God's love for us, to love others (Matthew 22:36-39).
- God's will is for us to draw attention to him and honor him by the way we live (1 Corinthians 6:20).
- God's will is that we be sexually pure (1 Thessalonians 4:3).
- God's will is that we thank and praise him no matter what happens (1 Thessalonians 5:18).
- God wants us to ask him for wisdom (James 1:5). He delights in revealing his will to those who are willing to follow him.

- God wants our life to be above reproach so that others will have nothing bad to say about us (1 Peter 2:15).
- God's will sometimes includes suffering (1 Peter 4:19). The writer to the Hebrews said, "Even though Jesus was God's Son, he learned obedience from the things he suffered" (Hebrews 5:8). Suffering is the school where we learn to be obedient and grow.

In Ephesians 5:17 Paul says, "Don't act thoughtlessly, but try to understand what the Lord wants you to do." Knowing and understanding God's will are not always the same. Understanding God's will comes only as we obey. For example, a teenager may look at the principle about sexuality and say, "Why should I stay sexually pure? Everyone else is doing it. I don't understand why I have to say no, God!" But as that teenager stays pure, he will begin to understand why God says no to sex outside of marriage. Many times we say to God, "When I understand your instructions, then I'll follow them." God tells us, "Follow my instructions, and then you'll understand."

In Proverbs 3:5-6 we read: "Trust in the Lord with all your heart; do not depend on your own understanding. Seek his will in all you do, and he will direct your paths." This passage has a promise for the Christian who wants to know God's will, but these three conditions must first be met:

1. Trust in the Lord with all your heart.
2. Do not depend on your own understanding.
3. Seek his will in all you do.

Then comes the promise . . . "and he will direct your paths." If you keep an attitude of trust and availability, God will show you each day what to do.

Here are some practical aids for determining God's will in major decisions. You can go over these when you wrestle with questions about your future, your desires, and your relationships.

- *Pray about it.* Ask God to remind you of passages of Scripture that apply to your situation. And listen for his guidance. He delights in his children's seeking him, and he delights in answering their prayers.
- *Consider your convictions.* Does this decision agree with biblically based convictions?
- *Consider your circumstances.* God will probably not lead you to be a professional singer if you're tone-deaf! On the other hand, if you are terrific in science and you want to help people, maybe there is an open door to becoming a doctor.
- *Seek the advice of godly people.* God can lead you through their counsel.
- *Let the Scriptures be your guide.* Don't take verses out of context, but search the Scriptures wisely. Remember, God's will never contradicts his Word! If you are really serious about honoring and following God, he will show you what he wants you to do.

God wants to give us his wisdom and lead us, but sometimes we are stubborn. David quotes God's words to us. This is God's promise: "I will guide you along the best pathway for your life. I will advise you and watch over you. Do not be like a senseless horse or mule that needs a bit and bridle to keep it under control" (Psalm 32:8-9). God is saying, "Hey, don't be mule-headed! Be responsive to the nudges of the Spirit. Don't make me yank on the reins to get you turned in the right direction!"

Sometimes we pray and look to God for an answer but the answer doesn't come. Those times are tough. Almost all committed Christians experience this delay at some point in their life of faith. When this happens, we must make sure we don't assume that God doesn't care. He proved his care when he sent Christ to die on the cross for us. It may be that he wants to build something into our faith that can't come through quick answers to prayer. Maybe he wants to teach us to believe him even when we can't see results for a while. Or maybe he wants us to seek him instead of the answer (Psalm 27:7-8). And maybe he is making our faith more pure and strong as we continue to seek him. In Psalm 25 David writes: "Show me the path where I should walk, O Lord; point out the right road for me to follow. Lead me by your truth and teach me, for you are the God who saves me. All day long I put my hope in you" (Psalm 25:4-5).

A lot of young people I know really want to follow God, but some are afraid they might miss out on his best for their life. A pastor once told me, "Don't worry about missing God's will. He loves you too much to let that happen to one of his children who really wants to honor him!" That's good to hear!

Remembering this might help:
God's will never contradicts his Word!

5

Should I go to college? If I should, how do I pick the one that's best for me?

I HAD SCHOLARSHIPS TO GO to several different colleges—Baylor, North Texas State, and the University of Houston. But I went to the University of Houston for one reason: I wanted to stay near the girl I was dating. My parents were adamant about my getting away from home. (I wonder why!) But I didn't want to leave. (I guess they were really serious about getting me out of the house because a few months after I started going to college, they moved to Florida . . . without me!)

A college education isn't for everybody. Some teens want to pursue vocations that don't require a degree from a college or university. Other young people have responsibilities that prevent them from going to college. For example, they may need to help provide for their families. The decision about college should be based on a person's goals, opportunities, and responsibilities.

Many people who choose not to go to college, however, later regret that decision. For many high school graduates, getting a degree could open a lot of doors. Increasingly, the job market requires technical training. Some form of higher education has become a necessity for those who want careers in computers in the information age.

Many careers require not only a bachelor's degree but also an advanced degree (master's or doctorate). The job market is increasingly competitive, and the people with the higher degrees have an edge in getting the best jobs.

If you aren't sure that college is right for you or if finances are a problem, you can try a semester or two at a junior college near your home. That experience will show you whether or not continuing to pursue a degree is up your alley.

For some families, tradition plays a big role in determining where high school grads go to college. If your mom and dad went to the University of Kentucky, they may expect you to go there too. If their college experience was really meaningful, their expectations might be even stronger. (Maybe your mother was a cheerleader or your dad burned down the administration building during an antiwar protest!) They want you to have the best possible college years, and it is understandable for them to reflect on their own experiences. I'm not saying you have to go where your folks would like you to go. I'm only saying that this is one of the factors to consider. Ultimately your desires and your parents' money need to find some common ground!

People who didn't choose to go to college right out of high school and now have to provide for their family may choose a nontraditional degree path. Night school, correspondence courses, and co-op courses offer opportunities for a degree to those who still have to put in forty hours a week at work. This approach takes longer, but tens of thousands of students are finding new opportunities by getting degrees in nontraditional ways. In fact, many universities have more nontraditional students than traditional ones.

As you think and pray about college and the important decisions you'll need to make, here are some things to consider:

- your interests and aptitude
- your exposure to the career you plan to pursue
- your grades
- your College Board scores
- finances
- scholarship opportunities
- your ability, emotionally and spiritually, to "go it alone"
- the counsel of mature people, including your parents
- the advantages of in-state and out-of-state schools
- the advantages of Christian and secular schools
- reasons why junior college first might be good
- availability of a campus with a good Christian group to join (almost every college and university has Christian organizations, as well as great churches in the community)

It's during the college years that many young people make the three greatest choices of their life: master, mate, and mission. They decide whom they will follow, whom they will marry, and how their life will count for eternity. So the decision you make about college is a significant one.

If you are in high school, talk to your parents, your school counselor, your youth pastor, and other friends and adults who can help you dream about your future. Pray for God's guidance. Then go for it! Enjoy those college years to the max! Virtually any obstacle can be overcome if you trust God and if you are willing to be creative and work hard to see your dreams fulfilled. Remember, the important thing is to walk with God during the decision-making process. He'll lead you. You can count on that.

Remembering this might help:

The decision about college should be based on a person's goals, opportunities, and responsibilities.

6

How do I know if God is calling me into the ministry?

WHEN I WAS A TWENTY-ONE-YEAR-OLD college student, my great-grandmother died. I met my dad in New Orleans, and we rented a car to drive up to Mississippi for the funeral. On the drive, Dad said, "Son, you've got one more year of college left. What are you going to do? What's your purpose in life?"

I told him, "Well, Dad, it's simple. You told me to get a degree and go make a living—and quit asking you for money. That's what I plan to do."

He said, "Son, you're not catching it. Let me ask it a different way. Why did God create you?" I started to answer, but he interrupted, "No, I don't want you to answer me now. I want you to think about it."

After my great-grandmother's funeral, we went to the graveside, where someone asked me to sing. I had a ghetto blaster, so I punched "play." As I sang "It Is Well with My Soul," I looked at the people standing at my great-grandmother's open grave. People were crying. People were thinking about life and death—the meaning of their existence. At that moment God said to me, "Al, this is why I created you. This is what I want you to do with your life. I want you to touch people with your singing."

After the funeral I got back in the car with Dad. I said,

"Do you remember the question you asked me a couple of hours ago?" He nodded. Then I told him, "I know what the answer is."

He said, "Son, I don't want to know what the answer is. All I want to say to you is this: Whatever God has told you to do, go do it with all your heart, and your mom and I will support you."

Some Christians think that the only specific "calling" from God is to full-time vocational ministry, but that's not the case. Every believer needs to actively pursue God's will. If we listen and obey, some of us will be led by God into nursing, law, farming, business, and even music! We can serve Christ wholeheartedly no matter what vocation he leads us into.

Still, a committed Christian is wise to ask God, "Lord, do you want me to go into a full-time vocational ministry?" Almost a century ago, God moved in the hearts of students across America and England, and thousands went to distant lands as missionaries. This movement, called the Student Volunteer Movement, began when one hundred students attended a conference and signed a pledge that said simply, "It is my purpose, if God permits, to become a foreign missionary." In only a few years, the hundred had grown to thousands—the largest missionary expansion in church history!

These were the best and brightest students in both countries. "The Cambridge Seven" sailed to India. C. T. Studd, a great athlete of his day, left sports and sailed away to obscurity in Africa to tell people the gospel of Christ. He said, "If Christ be God and died for me, there's no sacrifice for him I can make which is too great." John Mott was a Phi Beta Kappa student at Cornell University. He had remarkable leadership ability and planned on a career in business, law, and politics. God, however, had other plans. Mott signed the pledge and soon became the chairman of the Student Volunteer Movement. In a few years thirty thousand young men and women responded to the call of God and the needs in the world. They sailed away from home and comfort to serve God in lands where the gospel had never been heard!

Today God is still looking for young men and women who will respond to his call to love him with all their heart and serve him anywhere and anytime he directs them. All of us need to have the open heart to say, "Lord, where you lead, I will follow." But few people have absolutely pure motives, even for serving Christ. Some go into professional, full-time ministry for the wrong reasons. Here are a few:

- Some people may have had an intense experience when they became Christians, and they want to maintain that "spiritual high." They think the ministry is as high as you can go with God.
- Some Christians don't understand who they are in Christ. They believe they have to perform to get God to accept them. The only way to really win God's approval, they think, is to make the "ultimate sacrifice" and go into the ministry.
- Sometimes it is not God's approval a person is trying to win as much as it is the approval of parents, a girlfriend or boyfriend, or someone else important to that person.
- If a person is trying to get rid of old guilt, sometimes going into the ministry and "giving it all up for Jesus" is the only way he feels he can even the score.
- If a person has failed in other vocations, the ministry may look like a place to hide. It may also seem like a safe place, away from the temptations and trash of the secular business world.

- People who are insecure and need admiration, authority, or hero worship sometimes look to the ministry as a way to have it all. The pulpit becomes a stage, and the position becomes a way to have power over people.

If you are considering a career in ministry, first search your heart honestly and see if you have one or more of the above impure motives. You can ask God to show you what is really in your heart. Reflect on Psalm 139:23-24: "Search me, O God, and know my heart; test me and know my thoughts. Point out anything in me that offends you, and lead me along the path of everlasting life."

Maybe you have just become a Christian. Or perhaps you have drifted away from your faith and now you're back with enthusiasm. Is God calling you into the ministry, or is the Lord just calling you to a new, holy lifestyle?

The world doesn't need more preachers. It needs more godly Christians. The call to vocational ministry is a special one. If God is calling, he'll let you know! The desire will burn brighter and brighter, and nothing will dim it. Even though you could be successful at other things, you'll know you couldn't be happy doing anything else. God will also confirm it to you through mature Christians.

My pastor, Brother John Morgan, told me, "If you can do anything else besides sing, go do it. But if singing is the only thing that honestly makes you happy, then pursue it with all your heart!"

One more thing: If God is calling you to the ministry, begin to minister now. Don't wait until after your education is complete. God's calling to vocational Christian service almost always comes when people are already involved in sharing their faith, loving the unlovely, and serving in some capacity. So start where you are and look for ways to serve the Lord today. That will be a good pattern for your life no matter where God leads you.

Remembering this might help:

If God is calling, he'll let you know!

7

The Bible can be pretty overwhelming to me. How can I get wisdom and direction from it?

WHEN I FIRST STARTED TO READ THE BIBLE, I got really discouraged because it seemed so huge, and it talked about stuff I'd never heard of before (like tabernacles, bronze snakes, and flaming chariots). The more familiar I have become with the Scriptures, the more I appreciate the beauty, mystery, and rock-solid truth I (yes, even I!) find there.

Some people approach the Bible as if it is a magic charm. They think just having it near them will bring them luck. And if they actually read it, they expect incredible luck to come their way!

Others look at the Scriptures as a collection of wonderful one-liners. When they are discouraged or need some direction, they close their eyes and open to a page at random. They point to a verse (any verse!) and believe that is God's word for them at that moment. (Try it sometime. It can be kind of funny. One guy first found: "Judas went out and hanged himself." Then he found the command: "Now go and do the same." I'm glad he didn't take that as "a word from the Lord"!)

When I was in high school, I asked a girl named Ginny Engvall for a date. To my surprise (and maybe hers, too), she said yes. I drove to her house and walked her out to the car. I asked her if I could pray for us, and she nodded. So I prayed for our date. Then I said, "You believe the Bible, don't you?"

She said, "Sure, I do."

I said, "Do you think you should obey everything it says?"

"Yes, of course," she replied as a quizzical look began to appear on her face. "Good," I said. "I want to read you a verse of Scripture we need to obey." I opened the Bible and read Romans 16:16: "Greet one another with a holy kiss" (NIV).

Ginny shook her head. "Al, that's not gonna work on me."

I thought it was a good try!

The Bible is a history of God's people, but it is much more than a history book. It is a collection of beautiful hymns, but it is far more than a songbook. It is full of moral and ethical instructions, but the Scriptures are much more profound than a book of moral codes. Beneath and beyond all these things, the Bible is God's message, communicating his love and his purposes to the people he loves. It is God speaking to *you!*

As the loving King who is our heavenly Father, God gives us a message that is sometimes encouraging and comforting. In Psalm 23, one of the most beloved passages in the Scriptures, David sang, "The Lord is my shepherd." Sometimes God's message for us is one of directives and warnings. Paul wrote to Timothy, "Run from anything that stimulates youthful lust" (2 Timothy 2:22). And sometimes we hear God's gracious promises: "Don't be afraid, for I am with you. . . . I will strengthen you. I will help you" (Isaiah 41:10).

No matter what we hope to get from the Bible, we need to read it with an attitude of humility and respect because God uses his Word to reach into our deepest thoughts and our most hidden attitudes. When he exposes these, he can heal, comfort, and change us. The writer to the Hebrews talked about the incredible power of Scripture: "For the word of God is full of living power. It is sharper than the sharpest knife, cutting deep into our innermost thoughts and desires. It exposes us for what we really are. Nothing in all creation can hide from him. Everything is naked and exposed before his eyes. This is the God to whom we must explain all that we have done" (Hebrews 4:12-13). So when you read the Bible, expect God to expose your hidden thoughts. Kind of scary, huh? It is— until you remember that he loves you and you can trust him to forgive, comfort, and give direction.

A college student once told me about when he became a Christian. He said the guy who led him to Christ encouraged him to go through 1 and 2 Timothy, listing every promise and command. The student was amazed at how relevant Paul's words were to his own life! You might try that too. You can use the letters to Timothy or go through Ephesians, Colossians, Matthew, or some other book you choose.

Another young person told me she uses a very simple but profound method of Bible study. She takes each part of 2 Timothy 3:16-17: "All Scripture is inspired by God and is useful to teach us what is true and to make us realize what is wrong in our lives. It straightens us out and teaches us to do what is right. It is God's way of preparing us in every way, fully equipped for every good thing God wants us to do." She then asks specific questions about whatever text she is studying. For instance, she might be studying Romans 12:9, "Don't just pretend that you love others. Really love them." So she asks herself:

- Teaches what is true: What does this passage teach me? (Who, what, when, where, why, and how?)
- Makes us realize what is wrong in our life: In what ways does my life not measure up to what God wants?

- Straightens us out: What am I going to do about it?
- Teaches us to do what is right: How do I get these changes to take root in my daily schedule?

She uses this Bible study method only a verse or a paragraph at a time. She may read several chapters each day, but then she focuses her attention on one verse or one paragraph that captures her heart. She told me, "God has used this kind of study to make the Scriptures so much more rich and real. He's used it to change my life!" Now that's an endorsement!

Whatever Bible study method you use, come to the Scriptures with an expectant heart and a willingness to respond to God's message to you. Remember, God wants to communicate with his children. His Word and his gentle speaking to your heart are always consistent with each other. Each time you open the book, ask God to speak to you. He will.

Remembering this might help:

Come to the Scriptures with an expectant heart and a willingness to respond.

Questions about God, Sin, and Salvation

Hope for the American Student

When you feel as if nobody cares and you need someone to talk to, call the HOPELINE: 1-800-394-4673.

A caring encourager will be on the line to offer you hope from a biblical perspective 24 hours a day, 7 days a week, 365 days a year.

"Every adult fully aware . . . every student receiving care!"

8

What does it mean to be "saved"?

THE TERM *SAVED* IS VERY FAMILIAR to some people but strange to others. It means "to be rescued." But rescued from what? Is anybody drowning? Is there a fire? Was there a wreck? Well . . . yes! You and I were drowning spiritually. We were in big trouble, and we needed to be rescued. That's exactly what God did for us.

It's not just really wicked, evil murderers and rapists who need God's forgiveness. All of us fall short. All of us need to be rescued. And there aren't two hundred ways or twenty ways or even two ways to be rescued. There's only one: Jesus Christ. These days it's cool to be spiritual, and it's cool to be open-minded about all the religions and philosophies out there. But on Judgment Day we won't care about being cool. We will care only about whether we have trusted in the one who has the power to save. All the others may promise, but only one delivers. Only Jesus Christ rescues.

We all need saving, and there's only one way to be saved. Let me explain.

If you go all the way back to where time began, you find in the book of Genesis (the first book in the Bible) these words: "In the beginning God created. . . ." The Bible says God created the entire universe, and then he made his highest creation—man and woman. God created Adam and Eve to be like him and live forever.

They had it all! A beautiful place to live. Everything they could possibly want or need. Perfect bodies, a perfect marriage, perfect communication, perfect sex, no pain or sickness or sorrow. But most important, they had a perfect relationship with God. As long as they stayed within God's boundaries, they had it all. There was only one thing God told them not to do—he said not to eat the fruit of a certain tree. Satan came into the Garden in the form of a serpent and tempted them to disobey God. Adam and Eve made a choice to rebel against what God told them. They chose to do things their way instead of God's way, thinking they knew what was best for them.

The instant they chose to rebel, sin and all its evil entered the world. Adam and Eve started to grow old, and death entered the world for the first time. Where the environment had been perfect, there was now suffering, pain, sickness, and disease. Worst of all, Adam and Eve became spiritually dead. Their friendship with God was cut off. At that point God could have said, "Forget it!" He could have wiped them out with a single word. But because God's love for us was so great, he immediately began to provide a way to reconcile people to himself—to make enemies into friends.

The Bible says that God chose the blood of one life to be a substitute payment for sin in another life. The writer to the Hebrews stated, "Without the shedding of blood, there is no forgiveness of sins" (Hebrews 9:22). Leviticus 17:11 says that blood represents life. The first thing God did after Adam and Eve sinned was to kill an animal. The skin from the animal covered their physical nakedness, and we might think of its blood as representing a spiritual covering—a temporary payment for their sin. God promised that one day he would send the perfect sacrifice to be the complete payment for their sin.

Justice requires that you pay for what you do wrong. Because God is just, he requires that sin be paid for once and for all. The only one qualified to pay for the sin of the world was someone who had never sinned himself. So two thousand years ago Jesus, God's own Son, left the splendor of heaven and came to the earth as a little baby. He was the only baby who ever asked to be born. For thirty-three years he walked and lived among people. He faced every temptation and experience of life without sinning. By his life he taught us how to live.

Jesus became that once-and-for-all sacrifice for sin—dying in your place and in mine to pay for our sin. Jesus is offering you a new life and a new beginning. He'll not only give you an exciting life here on this earth, but also one day he'll take you to heaven to be with him forever. You can receive Christ's payment for your sins. Then you will be forgiven and made right with God. Or you can choose to ignore Christ or reject him. If you ignore or reject him, you pay for your own sin in a horrible place the Bible calls hell, created for the devil and his demons.

The choice is yours. Salvation is a gift from God, but like any other gift, it does not become yours until you reach out and take it. How do you do that?

- *Admit you are a sinner in need of God's forgiveness.* Paul wrote, "For all have sinned; all fall short of God's glorious standard" (Romans 3:23). He also wrote to the believers in Rome, "For the wages of sin is death, but the free gift of God is eternal life through Christ Jesus our Lord" (Romans 6:23).
- *Repent of (turn away from) your sin.* (See Luke 13:3.) Thank God for his forgiveness.
- *Trust God to give you a new heart and eternal life.* Jesus told Nicodemus, "For God so loved the world that he gave his only Son, so that everyone who believes in him will not perish but have eternal life" (John 3:16).
- *Tell someone about your new commitment to Christ.* Paul wrote, "If you confess with your mouth that Jesus is Lord and believe in your heart that God raised him from the dead, you will be saved. For it is by believing in your heart that you are made right with God, and it is by confessing with your mouth that you are saved. . . . For 'Anyone who calls on the name of the Lord will be saved'" (Romans 10:9-10, 13).

Pray a prayer something like the one printed below. Remember, there's nothing magical about the words. What counts is what you mean in your heart.

> Lord Jesus, I know I am a sinner, and I know my sin must be paid for. I accept your death on the cross as payment for my sin. Please forgive me of all my sin—past, present, and future. Please come into my heart and save me. I give you my life and ask you to be my Lord and Savior. Help me to live for you. Thank you, Jesus, for saving me. Amen.

If you prayed that prayer and meant it, then Jesus did exactly what you asked him to do! You may not have seen lights flash or heard angels sing, but in a split second something miraculous and supernatural took place. You were saved!

You now have a new life in Christ, and it's important that you start out right. Share what has just happened to you with someone else. Begin to study God's Word. (The Gospel of John is a good place to start.) Find a Bible-teaching, Bible-preaching, and Bible-believing church where you can grow in your new faith. Ask God to show you the church where he wants you to become a member. Talk to him every day. He loves you so much and wants to spend time with you.

You have made the most important decision you will ever make. God bless you in your new life as a radical Christian! Give it all you've got!

Remembering this might help:

Only Jesus can rescue us from drowning spiritually.

9

I'm afraid of dying. What can relieve my fears?

PEOPLE ASK ME ALL THE TIME if I was afraid when the airplane was going down. They want to know if I was afraid of dying. To be honest, I wasn't afraid of dying, but I was terrified of the pain I was getting ready to experience. I've been much more scared of dying when I've been on roller coasters!

Sometime ago a man came to one of my Take Me to the Cross concerts, and he said, "Al, you shed some new light on the cross for me, and I want to thank you."

I responded, "Good. What was it?"

He said, "Every time I drive by a church and see the cross high up on the steeple, I hate it."

"Why is that?" I asked.

"Because it pictures God as so high and far out of reach. But your songs tell me that God is in our heart, not high and far away."

If God is not in our heart, we will certainly feel distant from him in moments of fear. We will feel as if the cross is out of reach. But if he is in our heart, as close as he can possibly be, we can know he will be with us . . . no matter what.

Some people are afraid of the agony of burning to death . . . or drowning . . . or being hacked to death by a masked intruder. (Maybe they've watched too many Stephen King movies!) And some people are afraid of what comes after the time when their heart stops beating. If you are afraid, ask yourself this question: "Am I afraid of the way I'm going to die . . . or of being dead?"

If you are afraid of the way you're going to die, you aren't alone. Unless you die in your sleep, dying usually involves two things: pain and the unknown. If you are a Christian, you have God's promise that he will be there to go through it with you. In Psalm 23:4 David said, "Even when I walk through the dark valley of death, I will not be afraid, for you are close beside me."

The fear of actually being dead is often a response to the anticipation of judgment. Each of us, the Bible states very clearly, deserves eternal condemnation because of our sin. But that's why Jesus came! To forgive us, assure us, and give us eternal life! We overcome the fear of this judgment by accepting Jesus as our personal Lord and Savior (see question #8). When you have the assurance that you belong to Jesus, your fear will disappear. Jesus told his followers, "I assure you, those who listen to my message and believe in God who sent me have eternal life. They will never be condemned for their sins, but they have already passed from death into life" (John 5:24). That's his promise. You can count on it.

Another thing that will make death less scary is understanding what heaven is like. Heaven, the Bible tells us, is the most beautiful place you can ever imagine. It is a real city where the streets are gold and the gates are made of precious stones (Revelation 21:18-21). You will have a mansion there. Jesus told his disciples: "There are many rooms in my Father's home, and I am going to prepare a place for you. If this were not so, I would tell you plainly" (John 14:2). There you will live forever, never to be sick or sad again. Your friends and family who know Christ will be there too. You will know all of them and enjoy them for eternity. And what's even more important, you will enjoy the smile of God all day every day for all eternity!

In heaven you will have a new body with none of the problems or limitations of the old one. Imagine eating and not getting fat! Or not being held back by gravity. How about flying and walking through walls? The Bible gives us only a glimpse of what it will be like, but we can be sure that heaven is a place of joy and perfect peace forever.

The thing that will really make heaven so great is that Jesus will be there. We will spend eternity with the one who died for us because he loved us so much. Now that is something to look forward to!

Remembering this might help:

When you have the assurance that you belong to Jesus, your fear will disappear.

10

I'm so busy. How can I carve out time to spend with God?

I STAY REALLY BUSY. Sometimes way too busy. A few years ago I finished working at the office late one afternoon and headed home. When I opened the door, I saw that my wife, Tracie, had a candlelit dinner on the table. She looked gorgeous! With my incredibly quick mind, I thought, *Did I miss something?* It took me only a few seconds to realize that I had forgotten our fourth wedding anniversary! To make matters worse, Tracie was totally kind and considerate. She didn't yell or blame or fuss. She said, "Since you didn't mention going out tonight, I decided to fix dinner here for our anniversary." Man, did I learn something that night about being too busy!

You can tell what people value by looking at the way they spend their time and their money. How would you feel if you had a good friend who never had any time for you? In the same way, if you say you love God with all your heart and yet don't take time to get to know him better, you probably love something else more.

The older you become, the busier you'll get and the more demanding life will be. This is a battle you will fight for the rest of your life. But here's something to keep in mind: *If you are too busy to spend time alone with God, you are busier than God intends for you to be!*

We always find time for things we consider important. Spending time with God can be the richest part of the day. Here are some reasons why it is valuable:

- It's an opportunity to meet with the most powerful and wisest One in all of the heavens or the earth. And he loves you more than you can possibly imagine! Think of it this way: You're going to spend time with the King, your heavenly Dad!
- It's a resting place for a hectic life. It's a chance to slow down and quietly get a fresh perspective on things. During those moments, you have a chance to catch your breath.
- It's an opportunity to release the worries you've been carrying. You can pour out your heart to God and tell him about your problems. He cares, he understands, and he can provide the answers.
- It's a way to get to know God, not just know about him. The more time you spend with him, the deeper your relationship will become.
- It's not just a discipline, but an act of love. It's an opportunity to express your love to your Father, Friend, Savior, and Lord.

You might be wondering, "But what do you do when you spend time with God?" Good question. What do you do with your best Christian friend? You talk to each other, enjoy doing things together, and sometimes just spend time together without talking. It can be the same way in your relationship with God. Here are some suggestions:

- *Be expectant.* Don't just read a few verses of the Bible, then close the book and run out the door. You are meeting with the God of the universe, who longs to communicate his love and wisdom to you! Pay attention. Something good is coming your way in this interaction with God!

- *Listen.* Jesus is called "the Word" in John, chapter one, so we know he wants to communicate with us, not just listen to us talk to him—prayer is a two-way street. We listen to God as we read the Bible, which is his message to us, and as we hear him speak to our heart, giving us messages that are always consistent with the Scriptures.

- *Be honest with God.* In Psalm 62:8 David says, "Trust in [God] at all times. Pour out your heart to him, for God is our refuge." He already knows everything we think and feel, so we might as well be honest with him. As we open up, we can receive his comfort and wisdom.

- *Pray for specific needs.* God delights in giving good gifts to his children. When we pray specifically, we are more thankful for his gifts. Some people keep a prayer diary to record their requests and the answers. While God always answers prayer, we need to remember that sometimes he says yes, sometimes he says no, and sometimes he says wait. But we can be confident that he has a good reason for his answers, even if we don't understand them at the time.

- *Study the Scriptures.* Paul wrote to his friend Timothy, "All Scripture is inspired by God and is useful" (2 Timothy 3:16), but some parts are more useful than others! Ask your youth pastor and your friends what books of the Bible they enjoy most. I suggest Matthew, Mark, Luke, John, Daniel, Genesis, and Paul's letters. The two books of Samuel, of Kings, and of Chronicles are histories of the nation of Israel—especially of David and his family. You might read those to see how God related to his people. Whatever you read, start by praying, *Lord, this is your Word to me. Speak to my heart as I read it today.* He will.

When you understand the benefits of having a devotional time, it will be easier to make the time. Decide how, when, and where you are going to have your time alone with God. Then plan for it. Watch out! Satan will do everything he can to trip you up. Don't shoot yourself in the foot either. For example, it isn't nearly as hard to get up in the morning if you go to bed at a decent hour the night before.

It usually takes forty-five days of doing something on a daily basis to develop a habit.[1] If you blow it and miss your quiet time, don't get discouraged. Just begin again. Satan would love to rob you of the joy of a quiet time by reminding you of how many you have missed. Don't look at God as if he were some heavenly police officer, someone who will punish you for messing up. He is the perfect, loving Father who waits for you with open arms.

Jesus told people that God "will give you all you need from day to day if you live for him and make the Kingdom of God your primary concern" (Matthew 6:33). Carving out time to pray, read, and listen to God is a great way to make his kingdom "your primary concern"!

Remembering this might help:

If you are too busy to spend time alone with God, you are busier than God intends for you to be!

NOTES

1. Al Denson's devotional *Take Me to the Cross* (Wheaton, Ill.: Tyndale House, 1997) will help you develop the habit of spending time with God.

11

If God is loving, why does he allow suffering?

RECENTLY WE WATCHED TRACIE'S grandmother die of ALS, Lou Gehrig's disease. Slowly. Painfully. It was hard, but I realized there are things I'm never going to understand.
A few months before she died, we went to visit Grandma. Tracie went to tell her grandma good-bye—probably for the last time. I took our bags out to the car. When I turned to go back in, I looked through the large picture window in the front of the house and saw Tracie with her grandmother.
I was looking over her grandmother's shoulder at Tracie, who was sobbing. I walked to the door and stopped. It broke my heart to see Tracie hurting like that. I thought, *Why, God? Why are you letting this happen?* After a few minutes, I went back inside. When I walked into the room, I sensed a tremendous amount of peace from Tracie's grandmother. She wasn't asking those "Why?" questions. She was looking forward to going to be with Jesus. She knew God!

People have debated the issue of God's sovereignty and man's suffering for a long time. Some have concluded that God isn't strong enough to stop suffering. In their view he wants to help, but he just can't. Another view (the one I believe) is that God is the sovereign Lord, and he can cause or prevent anything he wants to. He has chosen, however, to allow us to suffer the consequences of sin in the world.

Sometimes the consequences are related to specific sins—those of others or of ourselves.

When God created man and woman, he gave us a wonderful gift: a free will. God could have made us like puppets who have no choice but to dance when our Creator pulls our strings. But God's love for us is so great that he gave us a free will, which he will never, under any circumstances, take away from us. God wants us to be free to choose to love him.

God created man and woman to live forever. If they had obeyed God, Adam and Eve would never have grown old and died. He gave them a world that was perfect. No pain, sorrow, suffering, hate, war, violence, sickness, or death. All of these are a result of their sin.

When Adam and Eve chose to rebel, sin and all its consequences entered the world. As long as there are people who are choosing to sin, there will be sickness, disease, suffering, and death. God hates sin and all the heartache it brings. The evil and bad that is in the world is not his fault. The fault belongs to us. Sadly, many of us have chosen to rebel against God, so we experience the specific consequences of our own sins. Even if we're Christians, we sometimes slip and make rotten choices. When we do, we can experience God's forgiveness, but we will also experience the consequences of our behavior.

God warned Adam not to disobey and told him there would be terrible consequences if he did. God could have washed his hands of the whole human race when Adam and Eve ignored him and chose to sin. But he didn't. He loves us and cares about our suffering. The cross of Jesus is historical evidence of God's involvement in our pain. Because of Christ, we can have a completely new perspective on suffering. When Paul wrote to the Romans, he assured them, "We can rejoice, too, when we run into problems and trials, for we know that they are good for us—they help us learn to endure. And endurance develops strength of character in us, and character strengthens our confident expectation of salvation. And this expectation will not disappoint us. For we know how dearly God loves us, because he has given us the Holy Spirit to fill our hearts with his love" (Romans 5:3-5). As we trust God, he will use our suffering to strengthen our character and ultimately produce a deep, strong hope in us.

God is not a passive spectator of our pain. He suffers with us. God became a man to die a horrible death in order to pay for our wrong choices! Incredible! Jesus defeated our sin on the cross and one day soon will be coming back in power and glory. If you want to live with him in a place where there will be no more death or sorrow or crying or pain, then make sure you have trusted in Christ. John wrote about the hope that God's people can look forward to in heaven: "[God] will remove all of their sorrows, and there will be no more death or sorrow or crying or pain. For the old world and its evils are gone forever" (Revelation 21:4).

God is a good and loving Father who involves himself in our life. He knows and understands our hurt. God will take us in his arms and comfort us if we will let him.

Paul was a man who experienced a lot of suffering. Because of his love for Christ, he was beaten, imprisoned, whipped, stoned, and shipwrecked. Still, he didn't doubt God's goodness or his sovereignty. In fact, Paul realized that our suffering makes us more compassionate to others who are in pain. He wrote to the believers in Corinth: "All praise to the God and Father of our Lord Jesus Christ. He is the source of every mercy and the God who comforts us. He comforts us in all our troubles so that we can comfort others. When others are troubled, we will be able to give them the same comfort God has given us. You can be sure that the more we suffer for Christ, the more God will shower us with his comfort through Christ" (2 Corinthians 1:3-5).

We know these things about God: He is loving, strong, and wise. Using the free will that he has given us, we are the ones who have caused a lot of problems by our choices to sin. Sometimes those choices affect only us, but often they affect other people too. Even then, however, God can turn what is ugly and evil into something good and positive if we will trust him.

Remembering this might help:

Suffering is a consequence of sin. God suffers with us. He became a man to die a horrible death in order to pay for our wrong choices. Incredible!

Questions of Lifestyle and Character

Hope for the American Student

When you feel as if nobody
cares and you need someone
to talk to, call the HOPELINE:
1-800-394-4673.

A caring encourager will be
on the line to offer you hope
from a biblical perspective
24 hours a day, 7 days a week,
365 days a year.

"Every adult fully aware . . .
every student receiving care!"

12

I know it's wrong to use foul language, but I can't seem to stop. What can I do about it?

RECENTLY A STUDENT CONFIDED TO ME that on a school trip with his soccer team he cursed a lot and used filthy language. I know this young man is a Christian. In fact, he's a leader in his youth group. I asked him to tell me what he was feeling and thinking when he used that kind of language. He said, "Well, the other boys were doing it, and I just wanted to fit in." He knew it was wrong. In fact, talking to me was his way of doing what James wrote about: "Confess your sins to each other . . . so that you may be healed" (James 5:16).

These are some of the reasons people use foul language:

- *It sounds "cool."* Of course, that depends on your definition of "cool," doesn't it? But if you hang around people
  who smoke, you're more likely to smoke. If you hang
  with people who use filthy language, you're probably

going to start using it too. And if you spend time with people who love God, well . . . that rubs off just as much!

- *It's the way many adults and older kids talk.* Some of us grow up in families where foul language is the air we breathe. Maybe your mom or dad cusses a lot. Maybe your older brothers or sisters use that kind of language. Modeling is a big factor in influencing how we behave, but it doesn't force us to do anything. We still make our own choices.

- *It's a habit.* Some people use filthy language just because that has become their vocabulary. They don't know any other way to express themselves. That's sad but true.

In Matthew 12:34-36 Jesus said, "For whatever is in your heart determines what you say. A good person produces good words from a good heart, and an evil person produces evil words from an evil heart. And I tell you this, that you must give an account on judgment day of every idle word you speak."

What comes out of our mouth reveals what is in our heart. Here are some encouragements from God's Word:

- You can become new from the inside out! "Those who become Christians become new persons. They are not the same anymore, for the old life is gone. A new life has begun!" (2 Corinthians 5:17). Now that does not mean you will never sin again if you are a Christian, but it does mean that the Holy Spirit puts new desires in you. He also empowers you to live out those desires. Sometimes the reason people can't live the Christian life is that they are not really Christians. They haven't allowed Jesus to have control of their life, so they have no power.

- Your mind (and your mouth) can be washed, dry-cleaned, and sandblasted by the Word of God. Paul wrote, "Don't copy the behavior and customs of this world, but let God transform you into a new person by changing the way you think. Then you will know what God wants you to do, and you will know how good and pleasing and perfect his will really is" (Romans 12:2). What are you feeding your brain? Do you have a steady diet of movies, books, music, and friends who use filthy language? Garbage in, garbage out. Eliminate those things from your life. Begin now to let God transform your life—and your mouth—by renewing your mind with God's Word.
- God will give you words that are good and right if you focus on what's good and right. Paul wrote to the people in Philippi, "Fix your thoughts on what is true and honorable and right. Think about things that are pure and lovely and admirable. Think about things that are excellent and worthy of praise. Keep putting into practice all you learned from me and heard from me and saw me doing, and the God of peace will be with you" (Philippians 4:8-9).

Even if you have a filthy mouth and bad language has become a habit, you can change. Trust God, and make the hard choices to stop. Replace that vocabulary with good, wholesome, direct speech. If you claim to be a follower of Christ, you may be the only Bible some people will ever read! So ask God to help you change the way you talk. Begin to take in God's Word, and be careful about the people and things you expose yourself to.

When a friend of mine, Jeff Calhoun, was a little kid, he

wanted to impress his older brother. His brother taught him two phrases: "Hey, dude" and "If you don't like it, stick it."

One day Jeff was walking around the house calling his mother "Dude," calling his father "Dude," calling the dog, the postal carrier—everybody—"Dude."

His dad took him aside one day and said, "Jeff, come here. Son, don't use that word *dude* anymore. It makes you look stupid."

Jeff thought for a minute and said, "Well, Dad, if you don't like it, stick it!"

Jeff told me, "At that moment, I learned what the term 'attitude adjustment' meant!"

Remembering this might help:

Your mind (and your mouth) can be washed, dry-cleaned, and sandblasted by the Word of God.

13

Is it wrong to drink, smoke, or dip tobacco? How can I know what's right and what's wrong?

I AM THIRTY-SEVEN YEARS OLD, and to this day I have never had a drop of alcohol, a cigarette, or a dip of tobacco. The Scriptures are very clear that getting drunk is a sin. Proverbs 20:1 says, "Wine produces mockers; liquor leads to brawls. Whoever is led astray by drink cannot be wise." The Bible doesn't say that smoking or dipping is a sin (the writers of the Old and New Testaments didn't know what tobacco was), but Scripture clearly states that our body is sacred and should not be defiled by anything.

Young people want to drink, use drugs, smoke, and dip for a lot of reasons. Some want to experiment and feel the buzz. Some go far beyond that and get bombed to numb their emotional pain. Others use these things so they will fit in with their friends. Some do alcohol, drugs, or tobacco out of defiant anger toward their parents. They want to hurt their parents by their self-destructive behavior. Some people start using alcohol or tobacco because they've seen their parents or older brothers and sisters drink or smoke.

I encourage you to avoid these things because

> . . . *you belong to God.* "Don't you know that your body is the temple of the Holy Spirit, who lives in you

and was given to you by God? You do not belong to yourself, for God bought you with a high price. So you must honor God with your body" (1 Corinthians 6:19-20). Alcohol and tobacco cause a wide range of health disorders and relational problems. Alcohol is the major cause of death among young drivers. Treat God's temple with respect!

. . . *just as with the law of diminishing returns, the effect of a stimulant or depressant wears off with continued use.* A person has to use more just to keep the same effect. Over time, the person develops a tolerance. Then he's hooked. A lot of young people say, "That won't happen to me!" And a lot of them are wrong.

. . . *you need to be a good example to your Christian friends.* Paul made a commitment to avoid anything that could hurt another believer, even eating meat that had been sacrificed to idols: "You are sinning against Christ when you sin against other Christians by encouraging them to do something they believe is wrong. If what I eat is going to make another Christian sin, I will never eat meat again as long as I live—for I don't want to make another Christian stumble" (1 Corinthians 8:12-13).

There has never been a time in history when the world needed to see Jesus any more clearly than it does today. And there has never been a time in history when it was more difficult to recognize Christ in Christians than it is today. What is it that sets you apart from the rest of the world? How does your life show Jesus to others? How do people tell the difference between your life and the lives of teens who don't know him? What is different about the way you talk, the places you go, and the things you do?

Think about what it is that motivates you to do or not do certain things. How do you decide between right and wrong?

- *Is your conscience your guide?* God gave each of us a conscience to help us determine right and wrong, but our conscience has been clouded and corrupted by sin. It isn't always a good gauge of what is right. Proverbs 14:12 says, "There is a path before each person that seems right, but it ends in death." Sometimes you can't trust your judgment. You need to get the advice of a wise friend or youth pastor.

- *Do you follow what society says?* Do you make decisions based on the character and behavior of the society around you? what you see on TV, in the movies, and in magazines? what you hear in today's music? what your friends do? Not a good call!

- *Do you live according to the Christian culture around you?* Are other Christians your measuring stick for holiness? For example, if you see some Christians approving of homosexuality or abortion, does that make those things right, even though God's Word says they're wrong?

- *Do you depend on your parents to help you decide what to do?* Should you? Maybe . . . maybe not. It's dangerous to determine right and wrong solely on your parents' attitudes and actions unless they line up with the Word of God. Parents aren't perfect. Some parents don't know Christ. They do things that aren't godly. You need to be careful here.

God hasn't called you to be like the world around you, like other Christians, or like your parents. He has called you to be like himself. Paul wrote to the Christians at Ephesus, "Live a life filled with love for others, following the example of Christ, who loved you and gave himself as a sacrifice to take away your sins" (Ephesians 5:2).

God, our Creator, has set the standards for us so that we'll be safe and happy in the world he has given us. He shares his guidelines in his Word. But what about the areas of conduct where the Bible does not give a specific yes or no? Sometimes we have to decide issues by general biblical principles. Here are five ways to help you decide if something is right or wrong:

- Be willing to look honestly at the evidence against the topic. For example, alcohol kills brain cells, causes cancer, destroys internal organs, is a major cause of accidents and violence, and destroys marriages and homes. It is the number one killer among students in America. Sure, it gives you a buzz, but it's a killer.
- Make sure you are right with God so you can hear him speak to you through the Holy Spirit (see John 16:13).
- Ask yourself, "Is this thing or activity more important in my life than God?"
- Ask yourself, "Does this thing or activity help me serve Christ better?"
- Watch people around you who are involved in this activity, and see what effect it has on them.

Here are three questions to help you choose what's right:

1. How will this activity affect me? my body? my personality? my relationship to the Lord?

2. How will it affect the cause of Christ? Can I honestly ask God to bless this activity? Will it hurt or discredit my church—the body of Christ?
3. How will it affect others and the influence I have on them? Will it make it harder or easier for me to witness? Will it hurt someone else?

There was a young man who grew up in a Christian home where the parents felt social drinking was OK. They used alcohol in moderation, only occasionally taking a drink. The boy took his first drink at his parents' table when he was fifteen. There was just one difference—he couldn't drink occasionally. Alcohol began to be a way to escape, a way for him to cope. He became an alcoholic. His parents' social drinking had been a stumbling block to him. Because he respected them, he assumed if drinking was OK for them, it must be OK for him, too. It wasn't.

Remember, as you are deciding what is right or wrong, the decision will be determined by the depth of your relationship with Jesus. You may be saying, "But what about my rights?" The fact is that at the moment you accepted Christ, you gave all your rights to Jesus. You have no rights. That's why we call him "Lord." If you care more about your right to participate in the things of this world, then you may need to examine your relationship with Christ. True salvation always brings with it a desire to live for Christ (1 John 3:3). Do you have a desire to be like Jesus in your actions, your attitudes, and the way you talk? What you decide now will determine whether you will experience God's best or whether you will suffer the consequences of your sin.

Make the right choice!

Remembering this might help:

Ask yourself: "How will this activity affect me? the cause of Christ? others?"

14

How can I stop using drugs and alcohol?

IT STARTS INNOCENTLY ENOUGH. A beer with your older brother . . . a wine cooler at a party . . . a joint after school with a friend . . . an upper on a dare. Maybe the first one was fun . . . maybe not. But somehow it led to a second and a third. Pretty soon you were spending your allowance on it and lying to your parents to hide what you were doing. Later you might have stolen some money to buy dope to keep the kick alive. But something happened. It stopped being fun.

You need to get help if you are drinking alcohol or using drugs and

   . . . you can't quit on your own.
   . . . your circle of friends has changed.
   . . . your use has escalated to regular drinking or using.
   . . . you have to use or drink alcohol just to feel "normal."
   . . . you have unexplained (or poorly explained!) absences from school or work.
   . . . you are having mood swings.
   . . . your behavior is unpredictable.
   . . . you are lying or stealing.
   . . . you see changes in your sleep patterns or eating habits.
   . . . you have increasing health problems.

. . . you have a poor memory or a glazed expression.

. . . your pupils are nonreactive.

. . . you are overdosing or mixing drugs.

. . . you tried to stop and you experienced withdrawal
symptoms.

. . . you have suicidal or homicidal thoughts.

. . . you feel out of control.

It takes a lot of courage to admit you have a problem.
When you do that, you're halfway to recovery! There's hope!

Some people define courage as pushing somebody out of
the path of a speeding car. Sure, that's a form of courage.
It's the kind that's connected to an internal IV of adrenaline!
My definition of courage is having the guts to stand alone
for what is right. For example, when a friend says, "Hey,
here's a beer for you," and everybody looks to see how you'll
respond, you have the guts to stand alone and say no, thanks.
No adrenaline. Just guts.

*Courage is doing what you know you should do in spite
of your fear.* A sign of maturity is when you understand the
difference between things you fear and need to face and
things you fear and need to avoid.

Jesus once asked a paralyzed man, "Would you like to get
well?" (John 5:6). It seems like a silly question, but it isn't
at all. The truth is that there are people who don't want to
be healed. If they were free of their problem, then they would
have to face life and take responsibility like everyone else . . .
with no excuses. No more blaming failures on a problem. No
more blaming parents. No more escaping.

Admitting the truth about the mess you are in and your
need for help is your part of the battle. Jesus' part is to heal
you not only physically but spiritually and psychologically,

too. It's not enough simply to break an addiction. You need to find the root of it, and that's always a spiritual problem. What caused you to begin this self-destructive lifestyle? Unless you deal with the spiritual and emotional problems, you will never get free and stay free physically. The change must come from the inside out. If you leave out the spiritual and don't get Christ-centered, biblically based counsel, you are not getting at the heart of the problem. In John 8:32 Jesus says, "The truth will set you free." Jesus explains in John 14:6, "I am the . . . truth." He and he alone is your hope.

Right now, admit your problem to your parents, pastor, youth minister, or another Christian adult you trust. That person will help you take the next step.

The path to wholeness almost always has twists and turns, along with advances and setbacks; but remember that God is with you all the time. You can turn to him, even when things look darkest. He will be your light!

Remembering this might help:

It's not enough simply to break an addiction. You need to find the root of it, and that's always a spiritual problem.

15

How can I stop lying and gossiping?

A FRIEND OF MINE TOLD ME that when he was twenty-one he got physically involved with his girlfriend. One day she came to him and said, "I'm pregnant. I need $350 for an abortion." He gave her the money and offered to go with her, but she wouldn't let him go. They split up, and he thought he would never see her again.

Fourteen years later this girl called him. She said, "I need to apologize to you. Do you remember when I told you I needed $350 for an abortion?"

"How could I forget?"

"Well, I wasn't pregnant. I just needed some money, and I thought that was the only way you would give me money."

For fourteen years my friend had lived with the guilt of getting a girl pregnant and paying for an abortion—taking a life. Of course, the two of them shouldn't have been physically involved in the first place. But the girl's lie hurt my friend more deeply than she could ever have imagined.

A lady went to her pastor to ask for forgiveness for gossiping about him. The pastor told her he would forgive her, but he wanted her to do something. He gave her a bag of feathers. He asked her to go to the center of town and empty the bag into the wind, then come back to see him the next day. She did as she was asked and came back to the pastor's office the next morning. The pastor then asked this woman to do one more thing. "Go back to the center of town and pick up all the feathers you released," he said.

"But, Pastor," she said, "that's impossible! The feathers have all blown away."

"That's right," the pastor replied. "And just as there is no way to find all those feathers, there is no way to take back your careless words about me."

Ouch! I bet she got the point.

Sometimes we think that talking about people doesn't hurt anybody. "Telling about Susan getting dumped by her boyfriend is no big deal. After all—" we might excuse ourselves— "she laughed when it happened to me!" But lying and gossiping are sins. In fact, the Scriptures put them in the same list with murder! Proverbs 6:16-19 says, "There are six things the Lord hates—no, seven things he detests: haughty eyes, a lying tongue, hands that kill the innocent, a heart that plots evil, feet that race to do wrong, a false witness who pours out lies, a person who sows discord among brothers."

If gossip and lying are so destructive, why do so many people do these things? Here are a few reasons:

- *Lying is a way to protect ourselves.* We feel if we tell the truth, people won't like us. It seems that the only way to avoid rejection is to deny what we have done.

- *Exaggerating the truth makes good things a little bit better and bad things a little bit worse.* Sometimes we exaggerate to impress people or to make them feel sorry for us. It seems harmless enough . . . except that it is lying. This form of lying is destructive to the person you are talking to, as well as to you. It also dishonors God. It's sin.

Sometimes we think we need to make God look better when we talk to our non-Christian friends, so we stretch the truth a bit to make it seem that God is doing *really* big things. Some people call this "evangelastic." But God doesn't need our embellishing of the truth to work in somebody's heart. The Holy Spirit is perfectly capable of doing his thing without you or me stretching reality to make God look good. Tell the truth, and trust God to work.

- *Gossiping is a way to make ourselves look important.* If we are "in the know" about everybody, it makes us feel superior. Gossiping is a way to make ourselves look "good" by making others look bad. Cutting people down behind their back makes a gossip feel bigger. Do you know how you can tell if somebody is getting ready to tell you some gossip? If they start by saying, "Guess what I heard," you can be sure it's gossip!
- *Lying is a way to avoid responsibility for our actions or the consequences of those actions.* We hope nobody will find out. And if we get away with it, we're much more likely to do it again.

Whatever the reason, gossiping and lying can become bad habits that are hard to break. They are spiritual problems rooted in our insecurities.

The first step in attempting to break these habits is to admit your gossiping and lying to God. Confess your sin, thank God for his forgiveness, and make a conscious decision not to gossip or lie again. Repentance is hard, but it is necessary for these habits to be broken. Ask God to show you the underlying problems in your life that compel you to do these things. Ask him to heal those areas and give you the strength to change. Take it one day at a time, and thank God every time you control your tongue.

If you have a problem with lying and gossiping, I encourage you to talk to someone and ask to be held accountable. Have this friend, youth pastor, or counselor ask you regularly (daily at first, then weekly) if you have lied or gossiped. Yeah, that's a tough thing to do, but there's something really powerful about knowing somebody is going to ask you a question like that. Real Christian discipleship involves accountability— for reading the Bible, praying, and sharing your faith, as well as for overcoming the sins that take root in your life. Take the step of asking somebody to hold you accountable. You'll be glad you did!

Remembering this might help:

Ask God to heal the areas in your life that compel you to do these things and to give you the strength to change.

16

What's the big deal about the occult and satanism?

THE WORD *OCCULT* MEANS "hidden" or "secret." We are living in a time when millions of people—including a lot of young people—are spending enormous amounts of money, time, and effort in the occult. The occult is the world of hidden, mystic arts that draws in thousands of people. These people are usually curious about the spirit world, witchcraft, magic, or predicting the future.

After reviewing a list of occult practices, a young person looked up and said, "I've been involved in just about all of those." What kinds of things were on the list?

The occult can take various forms. Here are a few:

astral projection	Ouija board
table lifting	speaking in a trance
automatic writing	visionary dreams
telepathy	ghosts
materialization	clairvoyance
fortune-telling	tarot cards
palm reading	astrology
magic charms[1]	

Some of the signs that people are involved in satanism and the occult include

- sudden and unreasonable changes in mood
- aggressive, unrestrained expressions of hostility
- unnatural attachment to charms and fortune-telling
- extreme, enslaving habits of sexual immorality, perversions
- gross blasphemy and unashamed mockery

All of us, Christians and non-Christians alike, experience some of Satan's evil devices: temptation, deception, and lust. But some people have participated in activities that have opened the door to a much more sinister presence of evil—demonization, the actual presence of demons oppressing or possessing the person. These activities, or entry points, allow Satan and his demons to have access to the person's life and soul. The activities, such as using a Ouija board or playing Dungeons and Dragons, Myst, Riven, and other fantasy video games, may seem harmless at first; but soon the unthinking person is trapped in the web of evil.

If you haven't participated in any of these activities, thank God for his mercy and make a firm commitment not to even dabble in them. The door may look harmless, but the room is full of evil, torment, and lies.

If you have been involved in any of the occult practices, you have committed a serious sin against God. The way out is through confession, repentance, and trust in Jesus for the strength to change. Immediately break all ties to any occult activity. Find an empty garbage can and burn all the occult literature and symbols. James 4:7 says, "Humble yourselves before God. Resist the Devil, and he will flee from you."

Here are some specific steps to take:

1. **Talk to your youth pastor or pastor.** Ask this person to walk with you in the path of repentance and cleansing described here. It is important that a young person caught in satanism get the insight, support, and prayer of a strong believer, or he just might become too scared or deceived or discouraged to face the future.

2. **Verbally declare your faith in the Lord Jesus Christ.** Ask for his forgiveness for these sins, and acknowledge him as Lord and Savior. As a response of faith, thank him for setting you free.

3. **Renounce (by name) every occult practice, false religion, or cult you have participated in.** Do this out loud. Be specific.

4. **Then deny any allegiance to the devil, his demonic host, and the occult.** Do this out loud too.

5. **For strength and support from the Scriptures, read Ephesians 6:10-17 out loud.** As you do this, "put on" each piece of God's armor: "Be strong with the Lord's mighty power. Put on all of God's armor so that you will be able to stand firm against all strategies and tricks of the Devil. For we are not fighting against people made of flesh and blood, but against the evil rulers and authorities of the unseen world, against those mighty powers of darkness who rule this world, and against wicked spirits in the heavenly realms. Use every piece of God's armor to resist the enemy in the time of evil, so that after the battle you will still be standing firm. Stand your ground, putting on the sturdy belt of truth and the body armor

of God's righteousness. For shoes, put on the peace that comes from the Good News, so that you will be fully prepared. In every battle you will need faith as your shield to stop the fiery arrows aimed at you by Satan. Put on salvation as your helmet, and take the sword of the Spirit, which is the word of God." So

   . . . tell the truth. Don't exaggerate even a little bit.

   . . . have integrity. It reflects the righteousness God has given you.

   . . . stand strong for Christ, no matter how unpopular it may be.

   . . . trust God in the big things in your life, and trust him with the small stuff too.

   . . . watch the material you read, movies you see, videos you watch, and games you play. What we think about shapes who we become.

6. Then firmly state your resistance to satanic influence.
On the basis of Christ's authority, tell Satan to get lost. Use the following "prayer of resistance" whenever you feel afraid and sense the attack of evil forces:

> I renounce any and all allegiance I have ever given to Satan and his host of wicked spirits. I refuse to be influenced or intimidated by them. I refuse to be used by them in any way whatsoever. I reject their attacks upon my body, spirit, soul, and mind. I resist them in the name of my Lord and Master, Jesus Christ, the champion over evil. I stand secure in the power of Jesus. He defeated Satan and all his powers on the cross. I stand upon the promises of God's Word. In humble faith, I do here and now put on the whole armor of God, which enables me to stand firm against the tricks of the devil.

You may feel completely set free from evil influences, but you will probably experience Satan's attacks very soon. Satan doesn't like to lose! Experience God's cleansing, and continue to talk to a pastor or another strong Christian who is knowledgeable about spiritual warfare. Don't be afraid because "the [Holy] Spirit who lives in you is greater than [Satan,] the spirit who lives in the world" (1 John 4:4).

In Ephesians 5:11 Paul encourages Christians to "rebuke and expose" "the worthless deeds of evil and darkness." In other words, we're to expose the occult for what it really is: a religion that promotes worship of, and service to, Satan. We must influence those caught up in this wickedness to put their trust in Jesus Christ. Never, never, never come close to this evil yourself.

Other passages you may want to study include

- *Leviticus 19:31.* "Do not rely on mediums and psychics, for you will be defiled by them. I, the Lord, am your God."
- *Deuteronomy 12:30-31.* "Do not say, 'How do these nations worship their gods? I want to follow their example.' You must not do this to the Lord your God. These nations have committed many detestable acts that the Lord hates, all in the name of their gods. They have even burned their sons and daughters as sacrifices to their gods."
- *Galatians 5:19-21.* "When you follow the desires of your sinful nature, your lives will produce these evil results: sexual immorality, impure thoughts, eagerness for lustful pleasure, idolatry, participation in demonic activities, hostility, quarreling, jealousy, outbursts of anger, selfish ambition, divisions, the feeling that everyone is wrong

except those in your own little group, envy, drunkenness, wild parties, and other kinds of sin. Let me tell you again, as I have before, that anyone living that sort of life will not inherit the Kingdom of God."

- *Revelation 21:8.* "But cowards who turn away from me, and unbelievers, and the corrupt, and murderers, and the immoral, and those who practice witchcraft, and idol worshipers, and all liars—their doom is in the lake that burns with fire and sulfur. This is the second death."

Some rock groups advertise their connection with Satan. To be honest with you, sometimes I'm not sure if they really worship Satan or if they are using that as a promotional gimmick. Marilyn Manson has said his songs and his image, which connect him to Satan, help him sell more CDs and make more money. I don't think it's any more righteous to use the devil for marketing than it is to actually worship him. Both are from the pit of hell. In essence, satanism and the occult are the worship and glorification of self. Marilyn Manson is a very lonely man who wants attention and is getting it by promoting his extreme, destructive message.

Buster Soaries is a youth speaker. I sang at a See You at the Pole rally in Jasper, Alabama, where he spoke not long ago. He drew the line between the Christian faith and all the cults, occult, and world religions. Buster said, "I'll stop preaching. I'll stop telling people about Christ. I'll denounce God and deny Christ. In fact, I'll go back to every person I've ever told the good news of Jesus Christ and tell them I was wrong . . . if anybody will [and here he adapted a line from *Jerry McGuire*] *show me the body!* But you can't show me Christ's body . . . because he's been raised from the dead. And he's alive."

Remembering this might help:

Let me tell you again, as I have before, that anyone [who participates in demonic activities] will not inherit the Kingdom of God (Galatians 5:21).

NOTES

1. See Neil Anderson's *The Bondage Breaker* (Eugene, Ore.: Harvest House, 1990), 235.

17
How can I know if I have godly character?

AS I TRAVEL AROUND THE COUNTRY, one thing I have learned to appreciate is that a lot of young people are choosing to live for Christ—all day, every day, no matter what the risk, no matter what the cost. Man, I know it's not easy! You don't get a lot of encouragement to honor Christ in all you do and say. Just turn on the television or go to a movie. *Party of Five, 90210,* and *Scream 2* don't exactly promote wisdom and godliness, now do they? So I appreciate you for your commitment to follow Christ.

You might be thinking, *Al, how do you know I've made that commitment? Have you read my E-mail?*

I know because you're reading this book! People who aren't serious about the Lord wouldn't have bought it, and they sure wouldn't be reading it! You get my point?

We wear a lot of hats: student, son or daughter, sibling, team member, club member, friend, Christian, and so on. It's easy to develop different personalities for each of these roles, but a person's character can be measured by two things: consistency and integrity.

Do you know any two-faced people? (That's a laugh, isn't it? It's like asking if you know any two-footed people! Of course you do!) It's easy for any of us—including me—to act differently in different situations to please people and fit in.

But consistency shows a strong, godly character. I know a young lady who has lots of friends in her high school. She has friends on the drill team, on the basketball team, in student government, in her youth group, and in her classes. The remarkable thing about this girl is that she is herself around all these people. She doesn't change her values, her beliefs, the way she talks, or what she says about people in order to win approval. She is consistent. She has a godly character.

The other measure is integrity. Thomas McCauley has said, "The measure of a person's real character is what he would do if he would never be found out." That is a terrific test of integrity. How do we act when nobody is looking? Who are we in the dark? When we see the answers for a test sitting on the teacher's desk and we're sure nobody will notice if we look, do we look? Do we stretch the truth to impress people? Do we shade the truth to get out of trouble with our parents? The fear of getting caught is a powerful motivator, but a truer test is how we act when we know we won't get caught.

The measuring sticks the world most often uses to determine a person's value are beauty, brains, bucks, and brawn—the four b's. This is a cruel and unfair system because no one can meet all the standards all the time. Even if you could, it still wouldn't be good enough because the standards keep changing. Just about the time you think you're pretty enough, cool enough, smart enough, or strong enough, somebody comes along and raises the standards. The price changes, the style changes, somebody makes a better grade, breaks your record, or beats you up. You are left feeling empty—as if you don't measure up. Society says you have to be a cut above everybody else to prove you have value. Most of us feel that we can't compete, so we give up and fall into the trap of looking, acting, and being like everybody else just to fit in and be accepted. But being one of the crowd will never bring you happiness that lasts. When the crowd is gone and you're all alone, the only thing that will bring you peace and satisfaction is knowing that somehow you're different. You're not like everybody else. Character is who you are and who you choose to be.

The poet Edgar Guest wrote a poem called "Myself":

I have to live with myself, and so
I want to be fit for myself to know;
I want to be able as days go by
Always to look myself straight in the eye;
I don't want to stand with the setting sun
And hate myself for the things I've done.

I don't want to keep on a closet shelf
A lot of secrets about myself,
And fool myself as I come and go
Into thinking that nobody else will know
The kind of a man I really am.[1]

Integrity is not a given in any life. It is a choice you must make every day. That's how consistency and integrity come together. A person of character respects, values, and appreciates the things that really matter in life. What matters? Clothes? Cars? Prestige? Power? Jesus said about your heavenly Father, "He will give you all you need from day to day if you live for him and make the Kingdom of God your primary concern" (Matthew 6:33).

There are a lot of motivations for making the tough choices to walk with Christ and have a godly character. One of these is the promise that we will be rewarded in heaven someday for making good choices now (1 Corinthians 3:10-15). But we don't have to wait until we die to be glad we avoided temptation and walked with God. The book of Proverbs is full of statements telling us that a godly life will be full of joy, peace, strength, and meaning . . . and that we'll avoid all the crud—the natural consequences—of bad choices. But there's one more really good reason for following Christ and obeying him. Jesus told his disciples and us, "Those who obey my commandments are the ones who love me. And because they love me, my Father will love them, and I will love them. And I will reveal myself to each one of them" (John 14:21). How's that for a promise?! Jesus says we will experience intimacy with him if we choose to honor him in our thoughts, words, and actions.

A great life isn't a destination but a journey. It is a process of trying and failing and learning from mistakes. Just be sure your mistakes aren't the really big kind! A damaged reputation can be restored, but people will always look at where the crack was. It takes a long time to build a good reputation and only one wrong choice to destroy it.

Remembering this might help:

A person's character can be measured by two things: consistency and integrity.

NOTES

1. From the *Collected Verse of Edgar A. Guest* (Chicago: The Reilly and Lee Co., 1934).

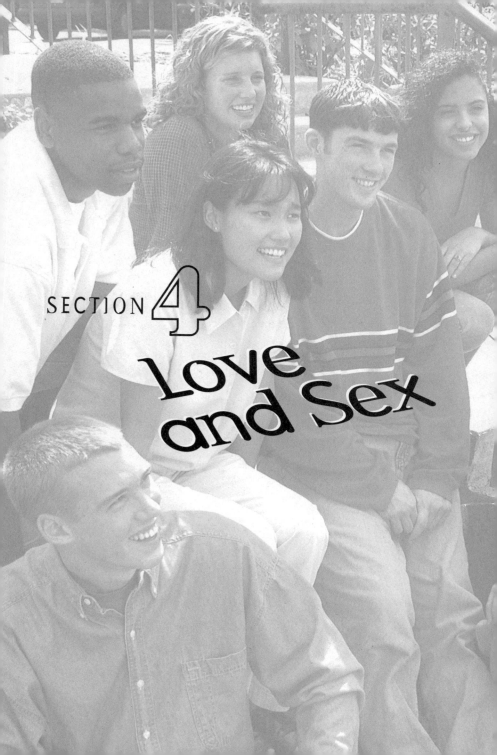

SECTION 4

Love
and Sex

Hope for the American Student

When you feel as if nobody cares and you need someone to talk to, call the HOPELINE: 1-800-394-4673.

A caring encourager will be on the line to offer you hope from a biblical perspective 24 hours a day, 7 days a week, 365 days a year.

"Every adult fully aware . . . every student receiving care!"

18

How can I know if I'm really in love?

GOOD QUESTION!

I was going to sing at a Valentine's banquet in California. Bill Hearne (of Sparrow Records) and his wife were coming to watch me because they were considering having me sign a contract for a record deal. I wanted to sing a particular love song I'd written, but I had to have a girl sing it with me, and I didn't know any California babes!

At 6:15 I was ready to rehearse. In walks this babe-and-a-half in a pink jumpsuit! I was thinking, *Wow! Check her out!* She looked at me, and she turned around and walked out. I thought, *Whoa! I'm not that ugly, am I?* A couple of minutes later she reappeared from a side door. She walked up onstage and introduced herself. We began learning the song together. I told her to sing it softly and romantically. (I was testing the waters!)

That night she and I sang the love song at the banquet.

While we were singing, God said, "Al, this is the girl I want you to marry."

Huh? Say what, God? OK, cool!

That's how I met Tracie, the girl who later did become my wife.

When *you* meet someone who may become your future spouse, do you think you'll know right away? Not necessarily. Sometimes God lets people know right away, but not always.

There is an emotion that can feel as strong as love, but it isn't love—it's infatuation. What is infatuation anyway? What's the difference between it and real love?

- *Infatuation is an emotion based largely on hormones, superficial attraction, and lust.* Real love is deeper than just emotion. Emotions can't always be trusted. They often change as circumstances around you change—for example, when you're sick, tired, stressed-out, fearful, and so on. Love is based on respect. It is a commitment to the other person whether the emotions are there or not. It is a type of devotion that will continue when the emotions aren't there.

David said he loved Kay and wanted to marry her when they graduated from college. Just before their senior year, Kay's face was scarred in an automobile accident. By Christmas, David broke off the engagement because he said he no longer loved Kay. What David felt wasn't real love that says, "I love you unconditionally, no matter what." It was an infatuation that said, "I cared because you were pretty (sexy, rich, popular, and so on)."

- *Infatuation is love at first sight—fireworks!—bells!—whistles!* You can be infatuated with someone you have never met, such as a movie star or someone you notice at school. Real love takes time. It's a growing experience based on shared interests, beliefs, and attitudes. Infatuation may lead to love over time, but it is not love.

- *Infatuation only takes; love gives.* Infatuation wants to know, "What is in this for me?" Love says, "What can I do for you? How can I help make you a success? How can I meet your needs?"
- *Infatuation is insecure.* It gets jealous and unreasonable. Love doesn't. Infatuation fades with time, separation, or change. Love won't. You've heard it said that "absence makes the heart grow fonder." Well, that is only true with real love. Being apart will kill infatuation over time because it must be fed regularly to survive. When someone else comes along who has more to give, infatuation will switch its attention from an old flame to a new one.

What is real love? The Bible uses Greek words to describe three different kinds: *eros* (sexual love), *phileo* (brotherly love), and *agape* (unconditional love). Too often we have the feelings of *eros* and think it's the real *agape* thing! We need to be careful that our hormones don't define what kind of love we express! God describes *agape* love in 1 Corinthians 13:4-7: "Love is patient and kind. Love is not jealous or boastful or proud or rude. Love does not demand its own way. Love is not irritable, and it keeps no record of when it has been wronged. It is never glad about injustice but rejoices whenever the truth wins out. Love never gives up, never loses faith, is always hopeful, and endures through every circumstance."

Compare your commitment to the real thing and see how you measure up.

- *Love is patient.* When you really love someone, you accept that person just as he is. Of course, you encourage him to grow, but you love and accept him unconditionally—no strings attached. Real love allows you to be patient with weaknesses and flaws.
- *Love is kind.* Love is positive and lifts people up, never pulls them down. Love sees the needs of others and does what it can to meet those needs. It's never harshly critical.
- *Love is not jealous.* Remember, love gives; it doesn't take. It wants to share time and attention with others. It allows the one you love the freedom to have friends and interests apart from you. It's not possessive.
- *Love is not boastful.* It allows you to center on the other person and not on yourself. If it brags about anything, it brags about the one you love.
- *Love is not proud.* Love keeps you from being full of yourself and keeps you humble. You are proud of your partner and not of yourself for snagging him or her. You realize that person is a gift from God, not somebody you have earned.
- *Love is not rude.* Love respects others and shows them courtesy. It demands respect from other people toward the one you love.
- *Love does not demand its own way.* Love thinks about others first. Real love accepts changes in circumstances and people. It produces a concern for the needs of others.
- *Love is not irritable.* It's not too sensitive or touchy. It doesn't take everything personally. Real love doesn't wear its feelings on a sleeve.
- *Love keeps no record of when it has been wronged.* It doesn't hold grudges. Love is able to forgive. It doesn't

dwell on past failures. In the Old Testament a teen named Joseph was sold into slavery by his older brothers. He was taken to a foreign country, never to see his home again. Many years later Joseph became the ruler of that country, which of course was Egypt. One day the brothers came to Egypt, begging for help but not knowing who was in charge. Joseph had a choice to make: forgive and help his brothers or hold a grudge and hurt them. What would you have done? Joseph said, "God turned into good what you meant for evil" (Genesis 50:20). Essentially he said, "I forgive you."

- *Love is never glad about injustice.* Real love doesn't find pleasure in the pain or wickedness of other people. It doesn't enjoy finding fault in others.
- *Love rejoices whenever the truth wins out.* Real love is based on truth and honesty. The Bible says that "perfect love expels all fear" (1 John 4:18). Fear is what keeps us from being honest. We fear what our friend will think of us or what she will do if she learns the truth. Love tells the truth even though it's not always pretty.
- *Love never gives up.* Love is loyal no matter what the cost. It will always stand by the person loved, no matter what.
- *Love never loses faith.* Love is willing to trust. When you really love someone, you'll believe in her, even when she cannot believe in herself. Again, because there is no fear in love, you trust that person. You're able to give yourself completely to the relationship.
- *Love is always hopeful.* It always expects the best and will always give a person the benefit of the doubt. Real love is positive, not negative. It looks for the best and finds it.

- *Love endures through every circumstance.* It survives all things and always stands its ground in defending the other person. Love is protective (without being jealous) and continues to love even if that love is not returned.

Now that's the real thing! How do your feelings of love compare with what God says love is? If you love someone, you should see the evidence. Real love can grow and mature if it's really there. Infatuation cannot produce the actions and attitudes of love. No matter how intense the feelings, it's not really love.

Remember, the Bible says that "God is love" (1 John 4:8). *To really know love and be able to love, we must know God.* As we learn to know him, we develop the desire and the power to love others—even those who don't seem too lovable! John wrote: "This is real love. It is not that we loved God, but that he loved us and sent his Son as a sacrifice to take away our sins. Dear friends, since God loved us that much, we surely ought to love each other. . . . If we love each other, God lives in us, and his love has been brought to full expression through us" (1 John 4:10-12).

God has to prepare you for marriage before he brings that person into your life. For me, he prepared me through a lot of broken relationships. I was a slow learner, but some things must have sunk in because God brought me the best in Tracie.

Remembering this might help:
Check to see if your feelings of love compare with what God says love is.

19

Is it wrong to have sex before you're married . . . if you really love the person?

IT SEEMS LIKE EVERY TIME you turn on the television, go to a movie, or open a magazine, you're bombarded with sex. Friends at school are "doing it"—even those you never dreamed would. Safe sex supposedly makes it right. But then you read that girls get pregnant and diseases such as AIDS are transmitted even with the use of condoms.

Many young people want to be free to experience sex. Most don't understand that there are significant consequences to pay for this kind of "freedom." It's important for you to know that the choices you make in this area will affect you for the rest of your life. It's like the man who wanted to sky-dive. He decided to be completely free, so he jumped out of the plane without a parachute. Soaring completely free without any restraints was great for a while—but he paid the price when he landed!

The Bible clearly teaches that it is wrong to go "all the way." Every time the word that's translated "fornication" in the King James Version appears in God's Word, it refers to premarital sex. Here are some of the verses about premarital sex, clarifying God's plan for sex and marriage:

- *Acts 15:20.* "We should write to them and tell them to abstain from eating meat sacrificed to idols, from sexual immorality, and from consuming blood or eating the meat of strangled animals."

- *1 Corinthians 6:13, 18.* "Our bodies were not made for sexual immorality. They were made for the Lord, and the Lord cares about our bodies. . . . Run away from sexual sin! No other sin so clearly affects the body as this one does. For sexual immorality is a sin against your own body."
- *Ephesians 5:3.* "Let there be no sexual immorality, impurity, or greed among you. Such sins have no place among God's people."
- *1 Thessalonians 4:3.* "God wants you to be holy, so you should keep clear of all sexual sin."
- *Hebrews 13:4.* "Give honor to marriage, and remain faithful to one another in marriage. God will surely judge people who are immoral and those who commit adultery."

God created sex for marriage only. In marriage, sex is totally awesome! Outside of marriage, sex will destroy your mate, yourself, and ultimately your relationship. The consequences of premarital sex are really serious. Here are just a few:

- *It robs you of your peace.* First Peter 2:11 says to "keep away from evil desires" that "fight against your very souls." The war raging inside you will be a result of the guilt, conviction, and unhappiness that come from crossing God's boundaries.
- *It damages your relationship with God.* Isaiah 59:2 says, "Your sins have cut you off from God. Because of your sin, he has turned away and will not listen anymore." Sexual sin causes you to lose your desire for spiritual things. There is no way to have a genuine interest in prayer, Bible study, witnessing, or worship for very long

if you are a slave to sexual sin. "For you are a slave to whatever controls you. And when people escape from the wicked ways of the world by learning about our Lord and Savior Jesus Christ and then get tangled up with sin and become its slave again, they are worse off than before" (2 Peter 2:19-20).

- *It will damage your usefulness to God.* 2 Timothy 2:21 says that "if you keep yourself pure, you will be a utensil God can use for his purpose. Your life will be clean, and you will be ready for the Master to use you for every good work." God will not use a dirty utensil. Only a person who is free from immorality can be useful in the kingdom. There's no way God will use you if you are not doing what his Word teaches. If your sin becomes public, it may cause others to stumble and dishonor the Lord's name. Even if you repent and get right with God, it will take time for people to trust you again.

- *It may damage your relationship with each other.* You may think physical involvement will bring you closer together, but it may drive you apart.

  1. *It can lead to a breakdown in communication.* If all you want to do when you are together is be physical, your verbal communication (the basis for rich interaction and understanding) will be seriously hindered.

  2. *It can also cause mistrust between the two of you.* Your partner may wonder, "If he will do this with me, who else has he done it with?"

  3. *It may lead to a loss of respect.* The farther you go physically, the more you lose your self-respect and your respect for the other person. You feel guilty, dirty, and unhappy with yourself and your partner for your lack of moral strength.

4. *It can lead to dishonesty.* When a guy has become sexually aroused, he will tell a girl almost anything to get her to lower her standards. If the only time your boyfriend says, "I love you," is when you are physically involved, watch out! You've become nothing more than a "good time."

5. *It will lead to loss of spiritual fellowship with one another.* You will not be able to talk about spiritual things. You may become bitter toward the other person and blame him or her for what has happened.

- *It may cause problems when you marry.* The couples who have the most problems after marriage are those who engaged in premarital sex. They're also the ones most likely to engage in adultery later.

- *You risk pregnancy, venereal disease, and AIDS.* Need I say more? Read the paper; watch TV; go to a clinic. You'll understand.

- *You will bring God's discipline upon yourself.* First Thessalonians 4:3-7 says, "God wants you to be holy, so you should keep clear of all sexual sin. . . . For the Lord avenges all such sins, as we have solemnly warned you before. God has called us to be holy, not to live impure lives." God always disciplines those who sin. Sexual immorality can destroy you and your partner.

Right now, ask God to help you keep yourself pure. First Corinthians 10:13 says, "Remember that the temptations that come into your life are no different from what others experience. And God is faithful. He will keep the temptation from becoming so strong that you can't stand up against it. When you are tempted, he will show you a way out so that you will not give in to it."

Remembering this might help:

The consequences of premarital sex are really serious.

20
How far is too far?

I DATED GINNY ENGVALL FOR FIVE and a half years, but things just didn't work out. Later, Ginny got married to a really cool guy named Jeff. I remember meeting Jeff. He said, "Al, I want to thank you."

"For what?" I asked him.

"For never having sex with Ginny all the years you two dated."

That made a big impact on me. I realized that my actions when I dated Ginny were continuing to affect not only Ginny and me but our spouses, our children, and our legacy for generations.

Two factors push young people too far. One is their desire to experiment—to try new things, to see what it feels like to do something new, different, and exciting. The second factor is hormones, the jet fuel of adolescence! I've seen a lot of young people who went too far too fast, and they deeply regretted it. They felt ashamed of themselves, trust in the other person was eroded or shattered, and they had a hard time getting over it. Or they just kept going down that slippery slope without looking back . . . and really got burned.

This is a controversial topic, but let me give you some guidelines I think are important:

- *Recognize that there is a progression.* Almost all couples begin by holding hands, then putting an arm around a shoulder, then putting an arm around the waist, then kissing, and on and on. Some know when to stop. Some don't.

- *Be aware that what feels good and satisfies one day may seem dull the next.* We want that rush, that feeling of excitement. And when it's gone, we want to go to the next level to get it back.

- *Know yourself.* Generally speaking, guys are turned on by sight, girls by touch. Girls, be aware that progressive touching will be harder and harder to stop. Guys, watch your minds! Learn to value character and heart, not just . . . well, you know.

- *Set limits.* Pray, talk to your youth pastor (or the youth pastor's spouse, if that's more comfortable for you), and get God's wisdom on how far to go. Set a limit on how far you will go on a particular date . . . before you get engaged . . . before you get married.

- *Learn to communicate verbally.* Too often a couple's communication becomes primarily physical instead of verbal. That ain't good! Instead of talking about problems, they kiss and hope the good feeling will just make the problem go away. Or they kiss instead of telling each other how much they appreciate each other. Don't let your physical expression get ahead of your ability to work through problems or to express affection with words.

- *Stay away from temptation.* Paul wrote to the Romans, "Let the Lord Jesus Christ take control of you, and don't think of ways to indulge your evil desires" (Romans 13:14). This means: Stay away from any and every situation where you might slip. Don't see how close you can come to the edge. Stay as far away as possible! Don't go parking on Lovers' Lane with a date who has a reputation for being "hot"! Don't go over to a date's house when nobody else is there. Be smart!

- *Honor the Lord.* Ask yourself at any moment: What will honor Christ, who bought me? Shift your focus away from seeing how far you can go to seeing how much you can please the Lord.

- *Seek what's best for the other person.* Instead of focusing on what thrills *you* can have, consider what is best for *the person you are with.* What will help that person grow in his or her relationship with Christ? How can you encourage that person in the faith—and not stimulate the person's hormones?

- *Go on group dates.* One of the best ways to get to know people and avoid sexual temptation is to go on group dates with Christian friends. And it's a lot of fun, too!

If you struggle with this problem (maybe you've already gone too far, or maybe your boyfriend or girlfriend wants more than you are willing to give), talk to your youth pastor, pastor, or a mature Christian friend. Remember, one day you will be married, and you will want to be at peace about how you conducted yourself in all your relationships up to that point.

Remembering this might help:

Shift your focus away from seeing how far you can go to seeing how much you can please the Lord.

21

My girlfriend is pregnant (or I'm pregnant)! What should I do?

THE FIRST THING MOST PEOPLE DO in that situation is . . . panic! Unfortunately, too many young people react and make impulsive decisions they regret later.

Make a commitment to be calm and rational. You need to be honest about what you did, confess your sin, repent, get good input, and carefully decide about breaking up or seeking other options. Talk to your youth pastor or a Christian school counselor to get some perspective.

It's important to tell both sets of parents. What you have done privately is now a family affair. Remember, a crisis can bring out either the best in a person or the worst, so be prepared. There should be a meeting with both families (and maybe a Christian counselor) to discuss your options. Here are some to consider:

- *Get married.* Are you both old enough and mature enough to understand real love and commitment? How will you live? How will you support yourselves and this child? What kind of future will you have together? Keep in mind, though, that making it right doesn't always mean marrying. Marriage may be the worst solution for a couple that is young and immature.
- *Keep the baby without getting married.* Again, is the girl old enough and mature enough to accept the responsibility

of raising a child and putting it first in her life for the next eighteen-plus years? Are her parents willing and able to help take on the emotional and financial responsibility? You need to think of everyone involved.

- *Have the baby and give it up for adoption.* There are many Christian agencies that find loving, Christian families for babies like yours. These couples can offer your child everything that you can't. Most young women who make this very difficult decision learn the hard lessons from their experiences and carry on with their life. Some, however, are not able to cope with giving their baby up for adoption.

You may be wondering, "What about abortion?" Those who favor abortion talk about the "rights and freedom" of the mother. Well, those who are saved have given their rights to God and have agreed to let him be in charge. Abortion is a cowardly way to cover up the embarrassment of an unwanted pregnancy. It may seem like a quick fix for a problem, but in reality it creates more problems. It can cause emotional, spiritual, mental, and sometimes even physical scars that will last a lifetime. For a detailed look at the issue of abortion, see the next question, number 22.

After the panic from the initial shock of finding out about the pregnancy subsides, clearer heads will prevail. Then you will be able to consider the options of keeping the child, putting it up for adoption, or getting married. There is not one right answer for this difficult question. Each case is different. You'll need wise, unbiased biblical counsel from a Christian adult you can trust. If you need help in taking the first step to tell your parents, ask that person to go with you. The most important thing to remember is that God loves you and is here for you, no matter what you have done.

When I was in high school, a friend—I'll call her Tanya—called me on a Friday night. She said, "Al, I'm pregnant. I need your help. Will you come over and be with me when I tell my parents?"

I asked, "Who's the father?"

She told me who it was, and I told her I'd be at her house the next morning.

On Saturday morning I knocked on the door of her house. It was so early, her parents were still in bed. They got up, and we went into the kitchen. Tanya told her mom and dad, "I hate to tell you this, but I'm going to have a baby." Tanya was afraid her parents would explode. Her mom and dad both started crying; then Tanya started crying too. Her dad got up and hugged her. He said, "Honey, I'm so sorry you made a mistake. What can we do to help you?"

Tanya had that baby, and her parents adopted the child. Seven years later Tanya and the father of the baby married and are together today. During those seven years, the two sets of parents were pretty upset with each other, but after a while their tempers cooled. Today the two families love each other, and the little baby is growing up feeling loved, safe, and supported. It's a great story of God's working a miracle out of a wrong choice two teenagers made. I wish I could say all the stories end this well.

Remembering this might help:

You need to be honest about what you did, confess your sin, repent, get good input, and carefully discuss your options.

22
Is abortion wrong?

THE ORIGINAL SIN OF ADAM AND EVE was that they
wanted to be as powerful as God. Abortion involves that sin.
The Bible makes it very clear that God is the giver of life and
the only one qualified to decide when a life will end. Making
the decision to end your baby's life means you have set yourself up to be God.

Our Creator, God, also says clearly in Scripture, "Do not
murder" (Exodus 20:13). Abortion is killing babies. That's the
second sin involved.

God knows us and sees us before we are ever born. Each
of us, before we are completely formed physically, is a living
soul that is special to God. David wrote, "You made all the
delicate, inner parts of my body and knit me together in my
mother's womb. Thank you for making me so wonderfully
complex! Your workmanship is marvelous—and how well
I know it. You watched me as I was being formed in utter
seclusion, as I was woven together in the dark of the womb.
You saw me before I was born. Every day of my life was
recorded in your book. Every moment was laid out before
a single day had passed" (Psalm 139:13-16).

Virtually all arguments in the abortion controversy focus
on the issue of the personhood of the fetus. The Supreme
Court decision of *Roe v. Wade*—as well as scientific, medical,

ethical, and moral considerations—point to this as the watershed. Several factors should be considered when we think of the fetus as a person rather than just "a part of the mother's body" or "a blob of tissue, like a tumor."

The following material is based on Peter Kreeft's dramatic debate on the issues surrounding abortion:

> Each person possesses a complete and unique genetic code, just as each person possesses unique fingerprints. This code exists at the moment of conception. The spermatozoa and the ovum each are haploid; that is, they each contain half of the code. When they combine, the zygote is created, which is diploid, containing the full complement of genetic code.
>
> Some pro-choice advocates say that the fetus is simply "part of the mother," with no identity of its own. Therefore, since a woman has the right to do whatever she pleases with her body (within the law, of course), then she has the right to discard that particular part of her body.
>
> This argument breaks down with simple logic, however, when you consider that the fetus possesses arms and legs after only a few weeks of life. At that point, the mother is not said to have four arms and four legs, or in the case of twins, to have six arms and six legs. A woman pregnant with a male fetus is not said to have a penis for the time of her pregnancy. Therefore, the fetus is not "part of the mother."
>
> The many differences between the fetus and an adult are important factors to those who are pro-choice. They point to the size differences, the degree of development, the dependence of the fetus on its

mother, and the lack of mobility of the fetus relative to an adult.

These differences, however, are not morally relevant if the fetus is a person. A preadolescent is smaller, less developed physiologically, dependent, and less mobile than an adult, but killing a preadolescent is, if anything, a more horrible crime than killing an adult precisely because the preadolescent is more vulnerable. The same is true of the unborn.[1]

Women who have had abortions often experience the powerful dynamics of guilt, the need for forgiveness, and the process of grief. Unresolved hurt, grief, and anger can manifest themselves in major depression, post-traumatic stress disorder (PTSD), and related problems.

Those who have had abortions sometimes believe they have committed the unpardonable sin. The Scriptures, however, do not say that, for God's grace and forgiveness extend even to those who kill others. King David committed adultery with Bathsheba, conspired to have her husband killed, and lied to cover his sin. Still, when God confronted him, God accepted David's confession and repentance. Psalms 32 and 51 declare the freedom from guilt David experienced.

David described the personal consequences of trying to hide his sin: "When I refused to confess my sin, I was weak and miserable, and I groaned all day long. Day and night your hand of discipline was heavy on me. My strength evaporated like water in the summer heat" (Psalm 32:3-4). His intense sense of guilt led to weakness and depression.

After Nathan rebuked David, who then repented, David experienced the refreshing forgiveness of God. He wrote: "Oh, what joy for those whose rebellion is forgiven, whose sin is put out of sight! Yes, what joy for those whose record the Lord has cleared of sin, whose lives are lived in complete honesty!" (Psalm 32:1-2).

Our sin, though, usually involves serious consequences. Some women who have had abortions become infertile. Some become more susceptible to uterine diseases. There are people who claim that these problems are God's punishment. The belief that these difficulties are divine consequences of sin, however, may or may not be accurate. R. C. Sproul writes: "It would be wrong to conclude that suffering is always an indication of divine punishment. We would be equally wrong to assert that it is never an indication of divine punishment. All that can be said for sure is that it *may* be an indication of divine punishment."[2]

Confessing the sin of abortion brings the joy of forgiveness, but it also brings the realization of loss. The sense of grief over this loss may be connected to a number of issues, including the death of the child, the foolishness of the choice, the loss of self-respect, the rejection (or perceived rejection) of family or friends, and the ridicule or misunderstanding of pro-choice friends who see nothing wrong with the abortion.

The grief process may last for months or years. Gradually, rationalizing is substituted with stark reality; blaming is replaced by genuine sorrow; guilt is washed away by refreshing forgiveness; and sadness gives way to the realization that God is good and sovereign and that life is worth living.

The power of oppressive guilt is not limited to women who have had abortions. Doctors who perform the operation may also experience extreme guilt. Sproul relates a doctor's comments: "One doctor reported in the *New York Times* that she had to prepare herself emotionally and often endured a sleepless night before an abortion was scheduled: 'It's a very tough thing for a gynecologist to do,' she said. 'The emotions it arouses are so strong . . . that doctors don't talk to each other about it.' On one occasion, this same doctor collapsed on the floor, overcome by emotion, after performing an abortion."[3]

Life is precious to God—your life and your baby's. If you have already had an abortion, then know that your baby is in heaven now. God can forgive you and cleanse you of the guilt and shame you feel. Tell a Christian counselor or another adult you trust what has happened. Let that person help you deal with this heavy burden.

For more information, see *Critical Concerns for Christian Counselors* by McGee, Rothberg, Moorhead, and Springle (Friendswood, Tex.: Baxter Press, 1997).

Remembering this might help:

Life is precious to God—your life and your baby's.

NOTES

1. Kreeft, Peter, *The Unaborted Socrates* (Downers Grove, Ill.: InterVarsity, 1983), 41–57.
2. Sproul, R. C., *Abortion: A Rational Look at an Emotional Issue* (Colorado Springs, Colo.: NavPress, 1990), 142–143.
3. Ibid., 144.

23

Is masturbation wrong?

OK, LET'S MOVE ON. Next question?

Masturbation is one of the most controversial—and most widely practiced—behaviors among young people. According to some studies, over 90 percent of young men and 50 percent of young women experience the sexual self-pleasuring that involves some form of direct physical stimulation. Males usually begin by age thirteen, females by fourteen.

The Bible doesn't mention masturbation in any of the lists of sexual sins, but many pastors and other believers consider it sinful. Adolescents are experimenting with all kinds of new behaviors as they learn to become adults, and masturbation is the most basic form of sexual experimentation. Some other reasons young people engage in masturbation: They find it to be pleasurable, they want release for their hormonal urges, and they desire to escape emotional pain.

Movies, television, billboards, magazines, and the latest fashions scream about sex! Advertisers use sexually attractive models to hype absolutely everything because . . . sex sells! Sexual stimulation is everywhere we turn—it's difficult to escape the constant bombardment of arousal today. This, combined with the other factors, makes masturbation attractive to young people.

Young people face several problems regarding this issue:

- *Obsessing.* If you find yourself thinking constantly of sex, then masturbation is probably only one of your problems. Obsessive thoughts short-circuit the building of meaningful relationships with the opposite sex because people are seen as objects to fulfill our gratification.
- *Pornography.* A high percentage of young men use pornographic material as a stimulus in masturbation. Pornography degrades people—both the one portrayed and the viewer—and that displeases God.
- *Too frequent masturbation.* Even those who think masturbation is normal identify too much self-stimulation as being harmful. Of course, this problem often is tied directly to obsessive thoughts about sex and pornography.
- *Guilt.* Some young people experience intense feelings of guilt and shame over their masturbation . . . even if it is very infrequent. This guilt is its own form of obsession, focusing on how awful the person is. Some young people experience the double whammy of obsessing about sex *and* how awful they are for thinking about it or masturbating.

I want to affirm to you that your sexuality isn't dirty or sinful. God made you a sexual being, and sexual desires are a part of being a living, breathing person. Like any other part of our life, sexuality can become distorted and destructive. That happens if we obsessively pursue it to the exclusion of normal, healthy relationships or if we wallow in shame over it.

These are my suggestions:

- *Give thanks for your God-given sexuality.*
- *Avoid inappropriate sexual stimulation.* Don't go to movies that portray sexually stimulating scenes in living color—and twenty feet tall! Don't check out pornographic

sites on the Internet when your parents are out of the house. Not when they're in the house either! Don't read pornographic articles or look at sexually explicit pictures—anywhere, anytime.

- *Pray.* Ask God for help to honor him in all you do.
- *Get help if you need it.* If you can't control your compulsion to masturbate, you need to talk to your youth pastor, counselor, or another trusted adult to get some help.
- *Focus on good things.* Paul wrote to the believers in Philippi, "And now, dear brothers and sisters, let me say one more thing as I close this letter. Fix your thoughts on what is true and honorable and right. Think about things that are pure and lovely and admirable. Think about things that are excellent and worthy of praise" (Philippians 4:8). If you focus on the good things, you won't have time for thoughts that dishonor God, demean people, and are destructive to yourself.

Remembering this might help:

Sexuality can become distorted and destructive if we obsessively pursue it or if we wallow in shame over it.

24

I think I may be gay. What should I do?

NO SOCIAL ISSUE HAS BEEN AS effectively inserted into American culture in the past decade as homosexuality. Only a generation ago people rarely even spoke of homosexuality in public, but today tolerance of gays and promotion of the gay preference is commonplace on many television programs, in magazine articles, and in government policies. Homosexual actors, lawmakers, singers, and a host of other public figures have "come out of the closet." At the same time, the media blasts conservative Christian views as backward and hateful.

I'm saying all this to show that the media cons us into thinking that being gay is OK, even though the Bible says it's not. These conflicting perspectives confuse a lot of young people. If you're confused, you're not alone.

People who struggle with homosexuality often feel anxious or depressed about their thoughts and behavior. They may feel a tremendous sense of shame and guilt. Some also compulsively masturbate to relieve their sexual urges. Many experience severe family difficulties, which may either *cause* their sexual urges or be caused *by* these urges.

In his excellent book *Eros Defiled,* John White says the definition of homosexuality should focus on actions, not just on feelings, thoughts, or disposition. He writes: "A homosexual act is one designed to produce sexual orgasm between members of the same sex. A homosexual is a man or woman who engages in homosexual acts."[1]

Psychologist Les Parrott writes about several categories of homosexual behavior:

- *Experimental homosexuality* covers a wide range of adolescent experimentation, from comparing sex organs to intercourse with a same-sex partner.

- *Homosexual panic* is a common occurrence in teenagers in which a person experiences sexual arousal when he or she sees nude bodies, such as in a shower. This usually doesn't mean the person is homosexual. It often occurs because viewing nudity of either gender is a novelty for adolescents.

- *Reactive homosexuality* is the fear of heterosexual experiences. Homosexual experiences are seen as less threatening, even though the person actually prefers heterosexual relationships.

- *Preferential homosexuality* occurs in people who are attracted to both sexes. In this case, they choose same-sex relationships.

- *Obligatory homosexuality* is the complete absence of heterosexual urges. These people feel that they have no option but homosexuality as a sexual preference, even though they may have very good social relationships with the opposite gender.[2]

Many young people experience the first three types of homosexual behavior (experimental, panic, and reactive) and assume—or fear—they are gay when they definitely are not. The other types (preferential and obligatory) indicate a more definite leaning toward homosexuality and need to be addressed more comprehensively.

The debate rages in the media about the causes of homo-sexuality. Some studies indicate a strong genetic cause. However, the studies I've seen have been conducted by homo-sexuals, so the results are suspect. Many authorities say homosexuality is a learned behavior. Some cite severe family disruption as the primary cause. The classic explana-tion is that a male may have gender-preference problems because he had a distant or hostile father and an over-protective, controlling mother.

A very strong factor seems to be an early seduction by an older sibling, some other family member, or a neighbor. This traumatic and often confusing experience (pain mixed with the pleasure of being pursued and valued even if it's in a perverse way) can leave the young person with conflict-ing emotions and a confused identity. It can (but does not always) lead to a homosexual lifestyle.

No matter how people feel about the legitimacy of homo-sexuality, the Bible clearly states that it is sin. That means people can repent of it, experience God's forgiveness, and receive his power to change. Paul wrote to the believers in Corinth, who tended to accept almost any lifestyle, "Don't you know that those who do wrong will have no share in the Kingdom of God? Don't fool yourselves. Those who indulge in sexual sin, who are idol worshipers, adulterers, male prostitutes, homosexuals, thieves, greedy people, drunkards, abusers, and swindlers—none of these will have a share in the Kingdom of God. There was a time when some of you were just like that, but now your sins have been washed away, and you have been set apart for God. You have been made right with God because of what the Lord Jesus Christ and the Spirit of our God have done for

you" (1 Corinthians 6:9-11). Some of them had been homo-
sexuals, but God had changed their lives!

If you or somebody you love struggles with homosexuality,
it is very helpful to determine which of the five types described
is the problem. If the category is experimental or panic, it's
quite certain that the person is not actually gay. The solution
is to limit these experiences as much as possible.

If the problem is reactive homosexual behavior, counseling
is recommended to help the person relate more effectively to
those of the opposite sex. This will reduce the anxiety and the
fear of relating to them.

If you, a friend, or a family member is struggling with preferential or obligatory homosexuality, professional counseling
is a must. Ask God to lead you to a Christian who is skilled
in this area and who will help the whole family deal with
the often explosive fear and anger, as well as the hopes and
expectations in all members of the family.

You might want to read other passages of Scripture that
deal with this issue:

—Genesis 1:28; 2:24; 19:4-9
—Leviticus 18:6-22
—Matthew 19:4-5
—Romans 1:24-28
—1 Corinthians 6:19-20
—1 Timothy 1:8-11
—2 Peter 2:1-22

Be careful to watch what you watch. Don't look at television programs or movies that promote tolerance of what the
Scriptures say is sin. That isn't healthy! But also remember:
God's grace is greater than any sin, and his power can change
the most darkened heart.

It's reassuring to know that many young people who fear they are gay really aren't at all. They need only to avoid the situations that cause them problems. Others, however, need the truth of the Word of God and the counsel of the body of Christ to get out of the entanglement of a homosexual lifestyle.

Remembering this might help:

Determine which type of homosexuality you are struggling with, and seek God's power to make the necessary changes in your lifestyle.

NOTES
1. John White, *Eros Defiled* (Downers Grove, Ill.: InterVarsity, 1977), 105.
2. Les Parrott III, *Helping the Struggling Adolescent* (Grand Rapids, Mich.: Zondervan, 1993), 152–161.

25

What's the harm in looking at a little skin?

OK, LET'S GET TO THE BOTTOM LINE at the beginning: Pornography is a substitute for real relationships. A very poor substitute. "Looking at a little skin" breeds fantasies that take us away from real people and real relationships. The unrealistic expectations these fantasies produce get in the way of genuine friendships and genuine love.

One of the things I've noticed in the past few years is that pornography and overt sexual talk is no longer the private domain of guys. While pornography is a bigger problem for guys than for girls, both need to be careful about what is feeding their mind.

I don't have to tell you that we live in a highly sexualized society. Almost everywhere sex seems to be the focus.

Listen to the radio. Unless your dial is tuned to a station that plays good Christian music, most of the songs you hear are about unmarried people "making it."

Turn on the television. Dramas are full of sex. Sitcoms make jokes of sexual encounters, almost always between unmarried people. And some of the most popular new shows have characters—guys and girls together—talking about penis sizes and orgasms. *SNL, Mad TV,* and other comedies use sex as common stock for laughs.

In the past few years, more and more movies have been

given an R rating because of sex. And we've gotten used to it. These days it's not uncommon for a group of kids from a youth group to go watch a movie full of sexual content!

The Internet gives people a unique opportunity to look at skin. It may take some creativity for teenagers to find somebody old enough to buy a *Playboy* or *Hustler* for them, but even kids can access all kinds of smut on their computers in the safety and privacy of their rooms. A friend of mine was doing some research about teenagers and soon was in the middle of scores of listings of teenage pornography sites, with the most graphic descriptions he had ever seen. You don't have to look for pornography to find it. This easy, private access has promoted the widespread popularity of videos and porn sites. The number of pornographic videos produced annually has increased dramatically since 1990.

In the teenage years, hormones don't just kick in. They begin to flame! The drive to have sex and the desire to fill your mind with images of naked bodies is really common. And it can get out of control very quickly! A lot of guys see how close to the flame they can get without getting burned . . . and pornography is so addictive that some of them end up not caring if they get burned.

Make no mistake—pornography is addictive. The more you see, the more you crave. The sights that satisfied a week ago don't give the same rush, so you have to find harder porn to satisfy the craving. It doesn't take long for you to lose sight of real people and begin living in a fantasy world. People who look at pornography learn to view women as things, not human beings.

One guy I know was hooked on pornography. He married a beautiful girl, but she couldn't measure up to the airbrushed babes in the magazines. What was his solution? He put a centerfold on the pillow so he could see it when he had sex with his wife. How do you think that made her feel?

Here are some ways to get away from the fantasies of pornography and find meaningful relationships:

1. **Thank God that you are normal!** Active hormones are a sign that you're healthy. Thank God for that. If you had no desire for sex, you'd have some really big problems. Thank God also for having a wonderful plan for your life, including your mental and emotional purity regarding sexuality.

2. **Make firm commitments.** By the time a guy picks up a copy of *Penthouse* and stares at the pages, he has made a series of choices: to feed his sex-sight appetite, to get a magazine, to find a secluded place to look at it ("Oh, I just like to read the articles." Yeah, right!), and probably to lie to his parents. Make commitments to

. . . honor the Lord in all you do.

. . . avoid staring at pretty women or macho men. (A friend says, "It's great to look once, but sin to look twice." When you stare, what's in your heart? Are you pursuing what's honoring to the Lord and best for that person? No, I didn't think so!)

. . . stay far, far away from television, movies, and magazines that show skin.

. . . build healthy friendships with the opposite sex.

3. **Be absorbed in Jesus.** I like the verse in Romans that says: "Let the Lord Jesus Christ take control of you, and don't think of ways to indulge your evil desires" (Romans 13:14). Be absorbed in Jesus, and don't even think at all about how to

get your sinful desires met. Another translation says, ". . . and make no provision for the flesh" (NASB). That means, don't put yourself in a place where you are tempted to sin. Stay away from porn sites on the Internet. Don't even get near a *Playboy* or *Penthouse*. And be really selective about what movies and television shows you watch. Yeah, I know that eliminates a lot of them. But being selective is a small price to pay for a lifetime of rich, rewarding relationships not colored by sexual fantasies.

4. Develop good friendships with the opposite sex. If you're a guy, the more pornography you see (soft porn on television and in most movies or hard porn in magazines, videos, and on the Internet), the more you will think of girls as objects instead of people. Put those things aside and develop really strong friendships—nonsexual friendships—with some girls. Don't kiss. Don't touch. Just talk. You might find out that some of them are pretty cool!

5. Treat people as if Jesus is right there next to you. Because he is! Remember that those naked figures in the videos and magazines, as well as the fully clothed ones sitting next to you in biology class, are people Jesus died for. That will help you stay away from pornography. And it will give you a different perspective on your role in the life of those sitting near you in class. God may use you to lead some of these friends to Christ or to encourage them in some positive, healthy way . . . if that's your heart's desire instead of using them to give you a few minutes of pleasure. Colossians 3:17 says: "And whatever you do or say, let it be as a representative of the Lord Jesus, all the while giving thanks through him to God the Father."

If you have a problem with pornography, talk to your youth pastor or someone else who can help you. Don't live any longer under the oppressive guilt of knowing that your thought life is out of control. Get the help you need. Your future wife and children will be glad you did. Really glad!

Remembering this might help:

Pornography breeds fantasies that take us away from real people and real relationships.

26

I'm in a relationship, but I know it's wrong. How can I get out?

YOU'VE ALREADY TAKEN THE FIRST STEP: admitting that the relationship isn't good. Lots of people stay . . . and stay . . . and stay in rotten relationships because they won't take that first step. Maybe they're afraid of letting go of the dream that this person will meet their romantic desires. Maybe you're afraid too. But at least you've taken that important first step!

Here are some things for you to consider now:

- *Think of the consequences.* One big motivation to leave a bad relationship is to think about what your life could be like a year, five years, or twenty years later. Not a pretty picture, huh? If that person is manipulating you through anger, guilt, or threats now, hey, things are probably only going to get worse. It's better to take the hard step now than to regret not taking it for the rest of your life.

- *Value yourself.* Most young people call a relationship "bad" because they feel belittled and controlled by the other person. Hey, you are a child of God, valuable and precious! It is your privilege (and your responsibility) to take care of your body and your life. These things belong to God, and he's entrusted it to you. Some people may try to control you by telling you how horrible you are or how you can't make it without them. Well . . . the fact of the matter is: You are terrific! And you certainly can make it. Actually, you can make it a lot better if you aren't hounded by a guiltmonger!

- *Have a plan.* Think about what you're going to say, how you're going to say it, and when "the event" will happen. Make it short and sweet, and be sure you know exactly how you are going to end the conversation as soon as you have cut the cord. The person may demand an explanation, but don't get hooked into a long, drawn-out discussion. Say, "This is my decision. And it's final."

- *Be strong.* In the minute before you cut off the relationship, you may think of a zillion reasons to stay and keep taking it. Be strong! Don't back down! The enemy of your soul wants to make you confused and weak so you will stay in a bad relationship, but don't listen to him.

- *Expect some heat.* In most cases, the person you are having a hard time breaking up with has used strong manipulation in the past to keep you hooked. He will probably turn up the heat now! Expect him to use guilt ("If you leave me, you're scum!"), self-pity ("Nobody loves me. I thought I could count on you, but now I'm so alone!"), rage ("@#$%^&!"), or threats ("If you break up with me, I'll tell everybody what we've been doing!"). Whatever he's used in the past, he'll use again to get you to come back. When he uses these manipulations, tell him, "It's exactly things like this that are the reasons we need to break up. I need somebody who doesn't try to use guilt (or rage or whatever) to control me, and you need some time alone so you can grow up."

- *Find a friend.* You'll probably need somebody to help you through this process. Be careful, though. You might confide in one of your friends about your desire to break up, but she may defend the guy instead of supporting you. Talk to your youth pastor, a volunteer, school counselor, or a mature friend you can trust to help you.
- *Make good friends.* Don't jump into the next relationship you can find. Take some time. Build some good friendships with guys and girls without allowing them to become exclusive and intimate. Take time to heal from the last relationship, or you just may find yourself making the same mistakes again and again. Hang out with people who respect you and value you, who don't try to control you. Hey, there are some of those folks out there—really!

Remembering this might help:

Value yourself, have a plan, and be strong—don't listen to the enemy of your soul.

27
What makes love last?

WOW! I COULD WRITE A WHOLE book on this one!

The day Tracie's grandfather and grandmother got married, her grandfather, Grandpa Barman, put a silver dollar in his pocket. He told me, "Al, there was never a day that I didn't have that silver dollar in my pocket. I kept it to remind me that God gave me a precious gift to take care of."

Recently, Tracie's grandmother died. Tracie asked me to get a present for her Grandpa Barman to show our love for them. I went to a store and bought a brand-new silver dollar. The image on it is an angel. We gave him the coin and told him, "This coin represents your angel, who is with Jesus now."

He told us, "You know, she was an angel even before she went to be with Jesus."

He put the old silver dollar in her hand in the casket, and he put the new one in his pocket. When I saw the strength of their love, it made me think about Tracie and me. Do we have what they had? I sure hope so. I sure think so.

A relationship develops staying power when it gradually moves from infatuation to real love. A lot of relationships between teenagers get started because of physical attraction, popularity, a "trophy" girl or guy (you know what I'm talking about!), or just the desire to avoid being alone. These reasons seem legitimate at the moment, but they won't stand the test of time . . . or the test of strain, which any relationship goes through.

Here are some characteristics of a good relationship that will last:

- *Communication—verbal, that is.* Two people who learn to speak their heart and work through problems have a much better chance of making it than a couple that tries to smooth over every rough spot by kissing . . . or anything more than kissing. Good verbal skills (and writing skills too) are essential to a lasting relationship. The goal here is to develop a genuine friendship as the bedrock of the communication. When two people really like each other, it shows!

- *Respect.* Two people who are dating almost always have a few things in common, but any couple has some friction points too. They need to respect their differences. How can you tell if there's respect? By the absence of sarcasm, ridicule, rolling eyes, sighs, and other signs that say, "I sure wish you'd change!"

- *Common interests.* Some relationships get started because of looks or popularity instead of common interests. However, if the two people enjoy two different sets of activities, their patience will eventually give out. Hormones will take a relationship only so far! Couples who genuinely enjoy doing things together have a better chance of developing a real friendship.

- *Affirmation.* Look for positive character qualities—such as integrity, honesty, courage, thankfulness, peace, and patience—and tell the person often what you see in him or her. Appreciating these qualities builds the other person's sense of esteem, and it builds the relationship, too.

- *Handling difficulties.* You really find out what kind of relationship you have (and what kind of person you are!) when your relationship is tested by difficulties. Solid, mature relationships are based on a strong commitment to each other, but they also aren't blindsided by the normal struggles of life. Here again, couples who can talk, share their feelings, and work out a solution have the best chance of growing through the problems. The relationship is hurt (maybe beyond repair) if one or both of the people explode, blame, withdraw, sulk, gossip, or demean the other person in some way.

Over the years I've seen a lot of relationships that have honored the Lord and encouraged the people involved, but I've also seen a lot (way too many!) that have hurt people. One of the biggest problems I've seen is "one-sided relation-ships." These are based on fear, not respect. One person domi-nates the other person and controls that person's behavior by demanding, yelling, pouting, or threatening to leave. The best thing the dominated person can do is let the domineering one go! But that's not what usually happens. The dominated person may be so afraid of being alone that he or she will put up with anything to stay in the relationship.

Another problem is jealousy. One (or both) feels insecure in the relationship and is threatened when the other person even talks to someone else. Of course, this threat is height-ened if someone is actually pursuing the person.

Here is a checklist to evaluate your dating and friendship relationships:

1. How did you resolve your last argument?
2. When you disagree, does one of you usually win? Who?

3. What haven't you said that you really *need* to say to the person?
4. How would your friends describe the relationship?
5. How do you respond when he (or she) talks to other girls (or guys)?
6. Where are you on the verbal skills vs. physical aspects of the relationship? Does anything need to change?
7. What character qualities do you appreciate about him or her?
8. What do you have in common? What interests and activities do you enjoy together?
9. Do you fear anything in the relationship? If so, what?
10. How complete are you without him or her?

A strong, healthy relationship occurs only between two strong, healthy people, not two people who desperately need each other (or somebody, whoever it may be!) to feel complete.

My good friend and youth pastor Emory Gadd once said, "The best way to *find* the right person is to *be* the right person." Focus on your relationship with the Lord. Grow strong in him. As you do, develop friendships with lots of people. Go on group dates, and when you date a particular person, focus on developing verbal communication skills, not kissing techniques!

Remembering this might help:

In a relationship that will last, two people learn to speak their heart; they respect their differences and really like each other!

SECTION 5

Friends and School

Hope for the American Student

When you feel as if nobody
cares and you need someone
to talk to, call the HOPELINE:
1-800-394-4673.

A caring encourager will be
on the line to offer you hope
from a biblical perspective
24 hours a day, 7 days a week,
365 days a year.

"Every adult fully aware . . .
every student receiving care!"

28

I spend all my time trying to please people, but I'm miserable! What can I do about it?

IT'S A GOOD THING TO BE PLEASANT and agreeable, but it's quite another to be a compulsive people pleaser. When we constantly change our opinions and behavior to fit in, we lose our sense of identity. And that makes us miserable. Underneath all the smiles and compliance is a deep, gnawing fear that we aren't good enough, we aren't acceptable, so we have to do whatever anybody wants. Some of us are so fearful that we read the slightest change in another person's tone of voice, the slightest raised eyebrow, or the slightest alteration in body language. Why? So we can quickly change our behavior to suit the other person. If you feel that you have to please people all the time, then you have a problem with *insecurity*.

In Luke 10 we see the story of someone who tried really hard to please people, but it made her miserable. Jesus was visiting his friends Mary and Martha, who were sisters. While Jesus was talking, Mary sat and listened. Martha didn't stop to listen. She "was worrying over the big dinner she was pre-paring" (Luke 10:40). In fact, she was really hacked off that she was busting her buns while her sister sat and listened to Jesus! And she was mad at Jesus for not fussing at Mary and telling her to help! She told him, "Lord, doesn't it seem unfair to you that my sister just sits here while I do all the work? Tell her to come and help me" (Luke 10:40).

Jesus didn't yell at Mary and tell her to get up and help. Instead he told Martha to get with the program: "My dear Martha, you are so upset over all these details! There is really only one thing worth being concerned about. Mary has discovered it—and I won't take it away from her" (Luke 10:41-42).

When we are insecure, we work like crazy to get people to like us, but it only makes us more lonely and angry . . . and more insecure. People who get caught up in trying to do things that will make everyone like them will never be happy.

Years ago my little brother finally got his driver's license, and he wanted to borrow Dad's car for a big date. Dad told him, "Son, I'll be glad to give you the keys to the car if you'll do one thing to please me."

"Sure. No problem. What's that, Dad?"

"You have to get a haircut."

My brother was stunned. "A haircut?! No way! That's not fair."

"No haircut, no keys."

My brother did the smart thing: He came to me for advice. I told him, "Hey, it's only ten o'clock in the morning. Dad will forget by six-thirty tonight. Don't cut your hair."

My brother liked my logic, so he had a smile on his face all day as he anticipated his big date that night. We washed the car that afternoon. Then he took a shower and put on some really nice-smelling cologne.

At six-thirty my brother walked into the living room and said, "Dad, I need the car keys now."

Dad looked at him and said, "Son, where are you going?"

"I'm going on my date."

"Son, don't you remember? I told you that you had to get a haircut before I'd let you have the car."

My brother was getting pretty freaked out. "But, Dad, that's not fair! I've got to leave for my date!"

Dad raised his voice. "Son, you're not walking out that door unless you can give me a really good reason for not getting your hair cut!"

My brother and I went back to our bedroom. I felt terrible because I was the one who had told him Dad would forget about the haircut. My brother looked at the big Bible Mom and Dad had given us because they wanted us to be like Jesus. It was open to a picture of Jesus . . . and Jesus had really long hair! My brother took the Bible into the living room and showed the picture to Dad. "Dad, here's a good reason right here! Jesus Christ had long hair!"

Dad smiled. "You're right, Son, and Jesus walked everywhere he went!"

Sometimes, no matter how hard you try to please, you're not going to get anywhere. Just ask my brother.

There is only one way you can truly be secure and have a healthy self-image. What way is that? Be aware that you are unconditionally loved and accepted by Jesus Christ, and understand who you are in him. What does that mean? It means you need to be sure you're a Christian. You need to be, as the apostle Paul said, "in Christ." Many Christians don't understand what happened to them the moment Christ saved them.

The Bible says the moment you took responsibility for your

sins and asked Jesus to forgive you, something supernatural happened. The "old you" died, and in its place was born a new person. Paul wrote to the Corinthians: "Therefore, if anyone is in Christ, he is a new creation; the old has gone, the new has come!" (2 Corinthians 5:17, NIV).

This "new you" may look like the "old you" on the outside, but inside (in your heart) everything is different. All your sins—past, present, and future—are forgiven, paid for by Christ's death on the cross. The Bible says you are holy, pure, and even blameless because of Jesus. Because God accepts Jesus, he accepts you for being "in Christ." Paul explained this a few verses later. He wrote about a fantastic swap that occurred the moment you trusted Christ. Christ took your sins, and he gave you his righteousness: "God made Christ, who never sinned, to be the offering for our sin, so that we could be made right with God through Christ" (2 Corinthians 5:21).

You give God pleasure. There is nothing you have to do to win his love or acceptance. He put his stamp of approval on you the moment you made a commitment to Christ as Savior and Lord. "God alone made it possible for you to be in Christ Jesus. For our benefit God made Christ to be wisdom itself. He is the one who made us acceptable to God. He made us pure and holy, and he gave himself to purchase our freedom" (1 Corinthians 1:30). He is thrilled that you are his!

Last year we put down new flooring in our kitchen. It was expensive, but it looked great! The same day the work was complete, we moved our refrigerator back into place. Even though we were super careful, we put two huge gashes in the new floor! We were sick! We tried to fix the floor, but we couldn't. So we went to the store and bought one of those country-style kitchen rugs to cover the cuts. The rug looks fine there, and no one else knows the floor was marred—but we know.

Many Christians think their life is like that floor. They are scarred by sin. The damage can't be repaired. To them, Jesus is like that rug. He just came along and covered their sin problem so who they really are doesn't show.

But that's not the way it is! The Bible says that Jesus doesn't just cover our sin—he supernaturally replaces the entire floor! He trades your torn-up life for a new, perfect one. There is no need to hide behind a rug or anything else. Since God accepts and loves you, you are free to love and accept yourself. The desperate need to please other people to win their approval gradually disappears. You already have God's approval, and that's all that matters!

What you think about yourself will determine how you live. If you think of yourself the way God does—loved, forgiven, pure, and blameless—then that is how you'll live. But if you still think of yourself like that scarred kitchen floor—a dirty, rotten sinner who could never change—then that is how you'll live.

There was a sixteen-year-old girl who started coming to our church several years ago. She had a bad reputation at her school, and she had earned it! Kathy had been sexually involved with several boys. When she came to us, she was a mess. She listened to the claims of Christ and received him as her Savior. Kathy was baptized and wanted to live for Jesus. She wanted to forget her past, but the kids at school wouldn't let her.

She was struggling. One night I sat down with her. "Kathy," I said, "do you understand that when God looks at you now, he doesn't see Kathy 'the tramp'? He doesn't see Kathy with all those guys. When God looks at you now, he sees Kathy, a beautiful, loved, forgiven young lady."

It was as if a lightbulb clicked on and a peace came to her. She just burst into tears. All she could say was, "Thank you, Jesus. Thank you, Jesus." From that day on, it didn't matter as much what others said. Kathy knew who she was in Christ, and she was free to serve the God who had set her free. She understood that because she was completely forgiven, she could forgive herself.

Right before the Civil War there was a godly man who lived in the South but hated slavery. He refused to own another human being. One day while he was in town, he noticed a slave auction going on. The man was usually sickened by the sight of these and stayed away, but that day something caught his eye. A husband, a wife, and a young child—a family—were about to be auctioned separately, never to see each other again. Their anxiety and grief cut him like a knife.

The man made his way to the front of the crowd just as the bidding started. He did something he had never done before—he bid first on the young father, then on the mother, then on the child. He had to pay a huge sum of money, but he purchased all three. The little family was so overwhelmed when they realized that they were going to get to stay together that they sobbed for joy.

The man paid his money and picked up the ownership papers. He walked over to where the three stood waiting in their chains. This man then ordered the chains removed and handed the papers to the astonished family. "Here," he told them. "I purchased you to set you free." These ex-slaves fell at his feet and said, "Master, we will serve you forever!" They did this not because they had to but out of an overwhelming sense of gratitude. They would gladly serve the one who had purchased them and bought their freedom.

When you understand what Christ did for you, you'll also want to serve the one who purchased your freedom. It makes sense. It's the logical response to the truth of Christ's incredible love! Pleasing him will *not* make you miserable, as trying to please people often does. But if you focus your attention on Christ, he will give you the security and the healthy self-image you need to have good relationships with people too.

Remembering this might help:

If you are a compulsive people pleaser, you have a problem with insecurity. You need to be aware that you are unconditionally loved and accepted by Jesus Christ.

29

What can I do when my friends reject me?

I DID ALL KINDS OF THINGS to make people like me in high school—letting the football team stuff me in a locker of smelly jocks and pretending I liked it; getting locked in a tuba case and shipped on the band bus; and doing all kinds of other stupid stuff—just so people would think I was cool. And sometimes they did.

But sometimes they didn't. And it hurt. Every year we went to band camp in Starkville, Mississippi. I played drums, and I always won the talent show. One year I didn't want to enter the talent show because I thought, *What if I don't win this year?* I was insecure. I was afraid of being rejected. So I didn't enter the talent show.

That night was the longest night of my high school life. I kept beating myself up during the show, asking, *Why am I just sitting here? Why didn't I enter the show? I'm so stupid! What's wrong with me?*

A friend of mine says, "I'm not afraid of rejection. I'm just tired of it!" Have you ever felt like that? I sure have.

All of us know the pain of rejection. Jesus himself felt the pain of being misunderstood, lied about, and ridiculed. The Scriptures say, "He was despised and rejected—a man of sorrows, acquainted with bitterest grief. We turned our backs on him and looked the other way when he went by. He was despised, and we did not care" (Isaiah 53:3).

The pain of feeling unwanted is one of the most awful experiences we can have. The message to us is: "You aren't valuable. You aren't loved." Sometimes this rejection is real. Other times it's imaginary. We may not feel good about ourselves, so we make the assumption that other people don't like us either. Then we misinterpret somebody's bad mood and think, *She hates me! She can't stand to be around me!* But in fact, the person's bad mood may have nothing at all to do with us!

Real or not, the experience of rejection is destructive if you respond in the wrong way. So what's the best way to deal with your feelings of rejection—feeling like you're on the outside looking in? First, decide whether you are going to believe what God says about you as a Christian (the truth) or if you are going to believe the lies Satan is selling (deception).

What is the truth? As a Christian you are forgiven, loved, and accepted by God. You are special, and you matter to God.

What is the deception? The lies Satan whispers in your ear sound like this: "You're a loser! No one likes you; nobody cares; you'll never change!" If you believe these lies, you'll probably experience feelings of worthlessness, depression, self-hatred, guilt, shame, despair, worry, doubt, fear, and hopelessness. You may even have thoughts of suicide.

Sometimes we get angry at God because he allows us to go through the pain of rejection. We think, *If God loved me, he wouldn't let this happen!* The psalmists, including David and Asaph, communicated this attitude from time to time, and to tell you the truth, I've felt that way myself. But the Scriptures are clear: "God showed [proved] his great love for us by sending Christ to die for us while we were still sinners" (Romans

5:8). We may feel that we're rejected by God, but that simply is not the case. He sometimes lets us go through painful experiences, but it is always for our good and growth.

Handling rejection comes down to a choice of your will. When you experience feelings of rejection: *Stop!* Take a few minutes to think: *Am I going to follow the truth of God or the deception of Satan?* You don't have to give in to those feelings of worthlessness based on the lies Satan hurls at you. If you need to, say out loud: "I choose to ignore Satan's lies about me. I choose to accept the truth about who God says I am. I am making this decision based on the facts and not on my current feelings." Then rehearse many times in your mind the truths of what God says about you and his love for you in the Bible. Reprogram the way you think about yourself, recalling verses such as these: "If God is for us, who can ever be against us? . . . Can anything ever separate us from Christ's love? Does it mean he no longer loves us if we have trouble or calamity, or are persecuted, or are hungry or cold or in danger or threatened with death? . . . No, despite all these things, overwhelming victory is ours through Christ, who loved us. And I am convinced that nothing can ever separate us from his love. Death can't, and life can't. The angels can't, and the demons can't. Our fears for today, our worries about tomorrow, and even the powers of hell can't keep God's love away. Whether we are high above the sky or in the deepest ocean, nothing in all creation will ever be able to separate us from the love of God that is revealed in Christ Jesus our Lord" (Romans 8:31, 35, 37-39).

David wrote about seeking encouragement from God's Word when he felt rejected: "I weep with grief; encourage me by your word. Keep me from lying to myself; give me the privilege of knowing your law. I have chosen to be faithful;

I have determined to live by your laws. I cling to your decrees. Lord, don't let me be put to shame!" (Psalm 119:28-31). As you take in God's Word and saturate yourself in it, feelings of rejection will become less of a problem for you! Remember, life is 10 percent what happens to us and 90 percent how we respond!

Don't try to be a Lone Ranger in this effort. Take the initiative to talk to your youth pastor or another mature Christian friend. Tell this person how you feel and ask him how he handles the pain of feeling rejected. If he says it's never a problem, find somebody else! He's living on Mars! But he won't say that because we all struggle—in some degree and in some way—when we feel unloved and unwanted.

God can use this experience to deepen your walk with him. When no one else understands, God does. When no one else cares, God does. When no one else has time for us, God does. When you can depend on no one else, you can depend on God.

Remembering this might help:

Life is 10 percent what happens to us and 90 percent how we respond!

30

I feel really lonely most of the time. What's wrong with me?

I HEAR THIS SAD COMMENT AND QUESTION more than any other. Loneliness must go with the territory of being a teenager. During these years we experience tremendous changes physically, mentally, emotionally, and socially. If everybody around us were stable, it would be hard enough; but our friends are going through the same things we are! When we go through the teen years, all of us try to figure out who we are and where our life is going. The pressure is enormous! So we say dumb things. We hurt each other, and we hurt ourselves.

In the struggle of learning to be independent, many teenagers have conflicts with the very people who are most committed to their welfare—their parents. Instead of seeing them as sources of comfort and encouragement, many teenagers see their parents as another source of pressure and mistrust. And they feel more alone because of that.

Lonely people tend to view authority the same way they view hurtful people in their life, especially if those people are parents. They are often intensely loyal to their parents, bosses, pastors, or other leaders. In their black-and-white perception (people or situations are either all right or all wrong, all good or all bad), they sometimes believe that the one in authority can do nothing wrong. They make others omnipotent because they feel so inadequate themselves. They will put up with all kinds of mistakes until, at last, the pendulum swings and the authority figure who could do nothing wrong suddenly can do nothing right.

Beneath this is the paradox that the lonely person wants to be accepted and appreciated by those who are in positions of importance and respect, so he values their opinions of him highly; in fact, too highly. But he also has an innate sense that those in authority are out to get him, to use him, and to manipulate him. Depending on which end of these extremes the pendulum has swung, he sees that authority as either black or white, either for or against him.

People often develop "masks" as a survival tool. When they were children, looking calm, cheerful, or tough enabled them to shield their feelings. These masks protected them in the past, but they are harmful in the long run because they prevent the development of honest and genuine relationships.

Lonely people desperately want to be understood and to feel close to others, but they're afraid. They're afraid to take the risks of involving themselves in relationships because they might be rejected. Then they would hurt even more. To avoid this risk, to avoid more pain, they protect themselves by appearing to be happy and well adjusted even when they are dying inside.

Hiding behind these masks, we don't say what we mean, and we don't mean what we say. To put it bluntly, we lie a lot. We say yes when we want to say no. We say we are just fine when we are feeling just a step or two away from suicide. We say we want to go somewhere we don't want to go at all because we think going there will make someone else like us.

We get so wrapped up in other people's desires that we get numb and confused and don't even know what we want! We are so busy making other people feel good that we don't know what *we* feel!

Some of us think, *The truth hurts, so avoid it. If people knew me, they'd reject me.* So we keep people from knowing how much we hurt and how angry we really are. We may protect ourselves from the risks of intimacy, but we feel very lonely. *When we lock others out, we lock ourselves in.*

Strangely, some of the most sociable people I know are also the most lonely. Sure, they're good at saying the clever thing or being cute or whatever, but they know they are just wearing a mask, playing a game. When they're alone, they wonder if people would accept them if they were ever honest and took the mask off. Maybe they've tried a time or two, and they got clobbered for being themselves. So the mask came back. And so did the doubts and the loneliness.

It's really important to pick your friends wisely. Maybe you need to find some new friends to hang out with. You need friends who can model what it means to gain your self-worth from the Lord and experience the freedom and motivation of the Christian life. This kind of friendship is rare, but there are people (including some you may not yet know) who can provide this environment for your growth. Look for friends who will affirm you, encourage you, be honest with you, and be good models for you. Then risk taking your mask off with these friends.

Scripture gives numerous admonitions and descriptions regarding relationships among believers. We are all part of the body of Christ, giving and receiving encouragement and strength from one another.

The writer to the Hebrews instructed them: "Think of ways to encourage one another to outbursts of love and good deeds. And let us not neglect our meeting together, as some people do, but encourage and warn each other, especially now that the day of his coming back again is drawing near" (Hebrews 10:24-25).

Jesus is a friend you can always trust. No matter what happens, he'll never disappoint you or let you down.

I sure wish I could have hung out with Jesus when he was walking around with his disciples. I would have loved to see the look in his eyes and hear the tone of his voice when he talked to people. But even though he's not here in the flesh right now, he's still here! And he is still just as loving and kind and fun! (Yes, fun. I think Jesus was the most fun person who ever lived. I can just see those folks sitting around a fire or in somebody's home or walking down the road having a great time together.)

Before he was crucified, Jesus spoke some very important things to his disciples. One of these was about his relationship with them. He told them, "I no longer call you servants, because a master doesn't confide in his servants. Now you are my friends, since I have told you everything the Father told me. You didn't choose me. I chose you. I appointed you to go and produce fruit that will last" (John 15:15-16). The God of the universe—the one who created everything and yet died to pay for our sins—calls you and me his friends! Cool!

I want to encourage you to find somebody you can talk to, somebody who will let you take off your mask and be real. Maybe that's your youth pastor, a counselor, or a mature friend you can trust. But it's always Jesus, too. You can be perfectly honest with him. You feel rejected? So did he. You feel misunderstood? He did also. You feel betrayed by those you trusted? So did Jesus. You want to find somebody who will love you unconditionally and who is kind and strong? He's waiting with open arms. He's always there for you. No, you can't see him, but you can know he's there because he said he would be. And he tells the truth. Always.

A businessman named Jerry walked the same path every day to work. His walk took him by an underpass where a group of homeless people lived. One day a man came up to him saying, "Hey, mister! Mister!"

Jerry told the man, "I don't have anything for you." And he stepped out to cross the street to get away from the man.

The guy called out, "That's not what I want, mister. What's your name?"

He stopped for just a second to look the man in the eyes; then he answered, "Jerry."

"Hi, Jerry. I'm Frank. Good to meet you."

Jerry nodded to him; then he quickly crossed the street.

A few days later Jerry was walking home from work when he noticed a crowd of people and an ambulance near the underpass. He asked what was going on, and an EMS attendant looked up and said, "A guy died."

Jerry looked over and saw who they were covering up. It was Frank. At that moment the attendant said, "Does anybody know this man?"

Jerry volunteered, "Yeah. His name is Frank."

"Oh, you know him?"

Jerry was a little bit embarrassed. "Yeah, I just met him one day on the way to work."

The attendant held out his hand with a bag in it. "Here are all his personal belongings. Since you knew him, you take them."

Jerry took the bag and went home. When he arrived, he opened the bag. He found some trash and some meaningless pieces of paper. He also found a file folder. The label on the top of the file folder read, "Friends." When he opened the folder, he found just one slip of paper. He looked at it. It said, "Jerry."

Sometimes we have no idea how a kind word and a minute of our time can touch the heart of a lonely person. Take the time to be a friend. I know how much it has meant to me for a friend or a stranger to take a minute to care.

If you help someone who is lonely, do you know what you'll discover? Your own feelings of loneliness will gradually begin to disappear!

Remembering this might help:

Lonely people desperately want to be understood and to feel close to others, but they're afraid to take the risks of involving themselves in relationships.

31

Are grades as important as my parents and teachers say they are?

GOOD GRADES ARE AN INVESTMENT in your future. They provide opportunities to go to colleges and universities (maybe even top schools), to get scholarships, and to get good jobs. However, good grades shouldn't be the top priority for Christians. Loving and obeying Christ are reserved for the top spot. Still, doing your best and getting the best grades you can are probably in the top five or so.

In my experience, the people who ask this question ("Are grades important?") are often in one of two camps: They either lack direction in their life or they are reacting (over-reacting?) to their parents' demands to study more and make better grades.

I've seen a lot of young people who go through slumps. Like a .320 hitter who goes one for thirty over several games, these students are temporarily bummed out, lethargic, direction-less. They have "lo mo" (low motivation). Usually, these are good students who are just burned out for a short time. Nothing to worry about . . . unless it becomes the norm.

Some other students are perpetually in a slump. (Like a .033 hitter who goes one for thirty! Consistent!) They lack direction. They don't care about their future. Actually, most young people like this have much bigger problems than their grade on Tuesday's algebra quiz. Their lack of direction and low motivation in school are symptoms of their desire to escape from pressure, stress, and responsibility at home. Strained family relationships sap their energies, and they can't muster the energy to study. They also tend to choose friends of like mind. These friends exert negative peer pressure on each other, which keeps all of them from breaking the mold and doing well in school.

On the other end of the spectrum are those students who are driven to do well and who are consumed with the need to excel in school. Sometimes their drive comes from some internal gyroscope that says, "You are scum if you don't make the top ten in your class!" And sometimes that message comes from their families. The fear of not meeting those high expectations propels them to study harder and demand more and more from themselves. It robs them of the joy of living. Even when they do well, they are satisfied for only a short while because . . . there's always tomorrow's chemistry test.

Both types of people (those with low motivation and those who are driven to excel) need to look deep inside and discover their underlying concerns. Both may be reacting to the fear of failure, but in opposite ways. Surfacing this hidden concern is the first step to finding a lasting solution.

Your study habits reflect your goals. If you want to go to a good college, you know that you'll need certain grades and Board scores. If you don't care where you go to college or if you don't plan to go beyond high school, you may not be too highly motivated to study hard and make good grades. Even if you have a low motivation level at this point or at some point in the future, I encourage you to take a long-range view. Be sure you make good enough grades to open doors and provide opportunities for the future if you decide later to pursue a more demanding college or career. But don't let anything come between you and your love for Christ. Keep a balance. Study hard. Play hard. And be radical in your love for Jesus!

Remembering this might help:

Be sure you make good enough grades to open doors and provide opportunities for the future.

32
Is it wrong to be competitive, to want to win in sports?

MOST PEOPLE QUIT TOO SOON. They get knocked down, and they think, *Man, that hurt! I think I'm going to quit.* The people who get up and keep trying are the heroes. Thomas Edison is known for inventing the lightbulb (and a lot of other great stuff), but he tried a bazillion things before he found something that worked. He had a great perspective. He said, "I'm making progress. I know a thousand ways it can't be done." We need that kind of perspective in every aspect of our life. There's nothing in the world wrong with having tenacity and courage . . . unless your tenacity is fueled by anger and a desperate need to prove yourself.

Sports has a higher profile in our culture today than ever before. Athletes make the news almost every night—some for helping the poor, some for fighting in bars, and some for making millions of dollars playing a kid's game. It's easy for young people to get caught up in all the hype and intensity of sports but miss out on the fun of competition.

I know a young lady on her school's basketball team who exemplifies the right attitude. I love to watch her play! When she's on the court, she gives everything she's got—110 percent at least. She dives for balls, goes for steals, rips down rebounds, and takes shots in the lane. Nobody questions her commitment to the team and to winning. But whenever a time-out is called, you can see a smile on her face. She constantly encourages other team members, even the ones who are competing for her position! And she makes friends with girls on the other team by talking to them as they line up for the rebound on foul shots. If she knocks down a player on the other team going for a rebound and a foul is called, she extends her hand to help her up. Everybody on the team knows this girl is a Christian, not just because she invites other players to youth group, but because of her actions.

Unfortunately, this young lady takes some flack from her coach and a few teammates who don't want her to be nice to people on the other team. A time or two one of the players has questioned her intensity because she is always so happy. (I guess being sullen and angry makes you a better player, huh?) But that doesn't make her stop. She's committed to honoring the Lord in all she does.

The question we need to ask ourselves is this: Is my attitude and behavior honoring to God? Paul wrote to the Corinthians, "Do all for the glory of God" (1 Corinthians 10:31). All. Not some. Not when it's convenient. All.

But that doesn't mean we don't do our best. Paul also wrote, "Work hard and cheerfully at whatever you do, as though you were working for the Lord rather than for people" (Colossians 3:23). This means we should be intense and play as hard as we can . . . as long as our first priority is to honor Christ.

Here are some ways to tell if your intensity is in the right place:

- Do you pray that your play and your attitude will honor Christ?
- Do you encourage people, or do you focus only on your own performance?

- How do you relate to players on the other team on the court or on the field? Do you try to intimidate them, ignore them, or befriend them?
- How do you treat people who fail? Do you condemn them or comfort them?
- Do you see the other team as enemies . . . or as people Christ died for?
- How do you respond when you win? when you lose?
- How do you respond when somebody from your school vandalizes another school? when your school is vandalized?
- Who are your sports heroes? Are they Christians who perform well and also have strong testimonies for Christ, or are they thugs who bully people?

Find other believers on your team (or on some other team at your school), and make a commitment to play and act the way God wants you to. When you blow it, confess it and do better next time.

Most young people don't play organized sports their whole life, but everyone relates to people day in and day out. See sports as a platform on which you can live out your testimony. Don't let winning be the main focus of your life.

Remembering this might help:

We should be intense and play as hard as we can . . . as long as our first priority is to honor Christ.

33

Some of my friends are pretty wild, but I really enjoy being with them. Is there a problem with that?

ONE TIME IN HIGH SCHOOL, the car I was in was pulled over by the police. A couple of the guys were drunk. Now I've never had a drop of alcohol in my life, but I was with guys who were wasted. These guys were just giving me a ride home from a party, but the police looked at me just like they looked at my friends. They made me walk the line and take the breath test just like the other guys. They assumed that I was drunk just because I was with people who were drunk.

We need to be careful that our reputation isn't colored by the people we associate with. On the other hand, we have a responsibility to show Jesus' love to every person everywhere.

When Jesus walked on earth, he related to all kinds of people. At one point, the religious leaders severely criticized him for being a friend to "outsiders"—tax collectors and prostitutes. The religious leaders knew Jesus had gone to parties with these folks and believed he had no business there! Jesus responded to the self-righteous leaders by saying, "Now go and learn the meaning of this Scripture: 'I want you to be merciful; I don't want your sacrifices.' For I have come to call sinners, not those who think they are already good enough" (Matthew 9:13).

Paul, too, was criticized for focusing his attention on all kinds of people. To defend himself, he wrote to the believers at Corinth,

> "I am not bound to obey people just because they pay me, yet I have become a servant of everyone so that I can bring them to Christ. When I am with the Jews, I become one of them so that I can bring them to Christ. . . . When I am with those who are oppressed, I share their oppression so that I might bring them to Christ. Yes, I try to find common ground with everyone so that I might bring them to Christ. I do all this to spread the Good News, and in doing so I enjoy its blessings" (1 Corinthians 9:19-23).

Would Jesus and Paul hang out with your wild friends? Absolutely! No question about it! But they would do it for a purpose: to help them become Christians. Did Jesus enjoy being with the tax collectors? You bet! That's why he was criticized. He didn't pronounce curses and judgment on them. Instead he loved them so they would listen.

Now, what about you and me? Sometimes we are attracted to the wild crowd because the things they do and the things they talk about seem so exciting. (And after all, sin is attractive. That's why we do sinful things!) But maturity is a vital ingredient. Jesus was the Lord of the universe. Paul was the leading evangelist of his day! Both of them were unquestionably solid and mature. They knew exactly why they were relating to people. You and I need to be a bit more careful.

Here are some questions about your relationship with your wild companions for you to consider:

- What is your attraction to these people?
- Are you sharing Christ with them? Do you intend to? When? How?
- Are you drifting away from your Christian friends as you develop relationships with the wild crowd?
- How will you draw these people into your youth group?
- Who is encouraging you to develop these relationships? Who is telling you to be careful?
- How is your desire to relate to the wild crowd affecting your relationship with Christ?

There's no doubt that somebody needs to tell these young people about Christ, as well as model his love and forgiveness to them. But I strongly encourage you to be clear about your purpose and to make sure somebody is doing it with you. Don't go alone. Even the apostle Paul didn't go on his mission trips alone. He always took a strong, mature friend with him. You should too.

A sophomore told me recently that he has lots of different types of friends—some in the youth group, some on his soccer team, some skaters, some potheads. He wondered if he was weird. I told him that it's a real strength to be able to relate to lots of different kinds of people . . . as long as you don't lose yourself in the process.

Make sure you don't compromise your beliefs or moral values as you relate to friends that most people consider pretty wild. Enjoy being their friend, but make sure they know where you stand. And spend some time alone with the mature Christian friend who is in this with you. Pray together, encourage each other, and hold each other accountable.

Then I know God will bless your friendships! That's the primary way the gospel is spread—one person caring enough about another person to tell him or her about Christ.

Remembering this might help:

Be clear about your purpose. Don't compromise your beliefs or moral values. Take a mature Christian friend with you.

34

I've messed up my life by making some really dumb choices. Now I don't think I can tell my friends about Jesus. What can I do?

WHEN I WAS SEVENTEEN, a nineteen-year-old friend called me and told me his girlfriend was pregnant. From that day on, this guy's life has never been the same because he felt he let his parents down, he let his brothers and his friends down, and he embarrassed himself. After four marriages, my friend is just living with a woman now, and his relationship with his family is cold and distant. He traces the downward slide of his life, which is a wreck, to that one event when he was nineteen.

One point is this: He made a mistake—a big mistake. But here is the second point: That mistake didn't have to ruin his life. Bad choices do three things: (1) They take you farther down the road than you want to walk; (2) they keep you longer than you want to stay; and (3) they cost you more than you want to pay.

We can't change the past, and we can't change how people react to us. However, every day we can choose how we will embrace that day. As I've said before, I am convinced that life is 10 percent what happens to me and 90 percent how I react to it. One of the greatest days in a person's life is when he stops blaming others for his problems and takes total responsibility for his attitude and behavior.

To me, one of the most comforting parts of the Bible is the description of when Peter proclaimed to Jesus that he would never forsake him. That very night Peter went out and denied Jesus three times. (No, that's not the comforting part yet!) Peter was heartbroken over his sin. The Scriptures say he cried "bitterly" (Matthew 26:75). But Jesus didn't reject Peter. (Now we're getting to the good part!) After the resurrection, Jesus allowed himself to be seen specifically by Peter (Luke 24:34). Later, when the disciples were having breakfast by the sea with Jesus, Christ gave Peter the opportunity to admit in front of his friends that he had repented and that he wanted to continue following Christ. Three times Jesus asked if Peter loved him— the same number of times Peter had denied Jesus. Peter was overcome with Jesus' love and forgiveness, each time responding, "You know I love you" (John 21:15-19). On the day of Pentecost, after Christ had gone back to heaven, Peter led three thousand people to Christ and became the leader of the early church.

My point is this: No matter how big your sin is, God's forgiveness is bigger. Don't give up on God or on yourself. If Jesus could forgive Peter for denying him three times and then use him to lead thousands of people to faith, just think what he can do for you.

Here are some questions for you to consider:

- Have you confessed your sin to Jesus, received his forgiveness, and allowed him to cleanse your life?
- Have you explained to your friends that you've not been giving them a clear picture of who Jesus really is?
- Have you seriously begun to make changes in your life and your lifestyle to show Jesus—and your friends—that you mean business?

- Have you forgiven yourself for your inconsistency and the things you have done?

It won't be easy to win the respect of your friends, but in time you can prove your sincerity. While a verbal witness for Christ is important, you need to back it up with how you live. Until you have established (or reestablished) your credibility as a Christian, the best thing you can do is to keep your mouth shut and walk the walk. Christianity is not just a set of facts you know—it's a way of life.

If you start being obedient to the Lord, how your friends respond to the gospel is not your responsibility. Success in witnessing about your faith to others will come from telling them clearly about Christ, trusting the Holy Spirit to work in their heart, and leaving the results to God.

Even if you've made some bad choices in the past, you can ask God to help you begin making good choices. It's important to know that the decisions you make today determine what's on the other side of tomorrow.

Remembering this might help:

If you seriously begin to make changes in your lifestyle, you'll show that you mean business.

35

We just moved to a new city, and I feel pretty awkward. What can I do to fit in?

THE AVERAGE FAMILY MOVES from one city to another four times. Unfortunately, this might happen when you're in high school! Awkward? Yes. Threatening? You bet. A wonderful opportunity? Sure.

Some of us don't have any problem at all moving to another city. It's time to blow Dodge and move on! But most of us dread moving and leaving the friends we've known.

As hard as it is, don't make it harder by blaming your parents. Your mom or dad probably couldn't help it. Maybe he was promoted. Maybe she needed a new job. Maybe they need to be nearer to your grandparents, especially if your grandparents aren't well. Blaming your parents won't help you fit in better, and it could make the whole transition a royal pain . . . for everybody!

When you get to a new city, don't wait around too long before you begin to start new relationships. Take the initiative to get to know people. Even if your family hasn't decided on a new church home, you can attend a youth group (or two or . . .) to meet people. Remember, when a new person comes into a group, it can be just as awkward for the regulars as it is for the new people. So why not take the first step and introduce yourself? As conversations develop, find somebody you enjoy and do something together: You could go to the mall, a movie, a ball game, a concert, a coffee shop, or whatever.

If school has started, take the initiative there, too. Talk to people. Ask them questions. Most people are really happy to tell you what they like and don't like about their town! You might join a club or a class organization to get to know more people.

Also be observant! Sometimes we feel needy when we show up in a new city. At that point, we tend to let our guard down. Instead, you should be careful to notice how other people relate to a person you've chosen to be with. You may have made a really good first choice of a relationship . . . or you may have blown it! Don't lock in on one person. Get to know a lot of people. If your new "friend" demands all your attention, watch out! That's a sure sign that you need to find some more friends.

Don't forget your friends back where you came from. Call, write, or E-mail to stay in touch. Tell your old friends about what's going on, and get their advice and encouragement. It's a good idea to have one (or more) of your old buddies come for a visit soon after you get to your new home, or maybe you can go back to see them. Those relationships are important and don't need to be severed. They just require a bit more work.

Moving to a new city can be one of the biggest opportunities of your life. In the new setting you aren't bound by others' fixed expectations of you. Try new things! (Within reason, of course!)

But moving also involves some risk. Here are a few dos and don'ts to consider:

- Don't let your anxiety and disappointment make you drop your guard.
- Don't do something stupid just to fit in!

- Remember to honor the Lord in all you do. He is sovereign over the affairs of kings and nations and over your life, too.
- Pray that God will lead you to new friends and a youth group where you'll feel loved and accepted and where you can minister to others.
- Let the awkwardness of the time deepen your walk with God as you pray more, depend on him more, and get more wisdom and strength from the Scriptures.

Your parents and brothers and sisters may also be going through a difficult transition. So try to look beyond yourself, finding ways to show that you care about the feelings and needs of the rest of your family. The move may create some difficulties, but it can also strengthen your family's communication and love for each other.

Remembering this might help:
Take the initiative to get to know people.

36

I have a friend who was sexually abused. How can I help her?

THIS IS AN EXPLOSIVE, DIFFICULT issue and too big a burden for you to carry alone. Be sure that you talk to your youth pastor, school counselor, or a mature Christian about the situation. If you have told your friend you would keep her comments confidential, you can tell her now that you aren't qualified to help by yourself. It is an awkward position, but she has come to you for help. Get her the help she needs! (By the way, women aren't the only ones who experience the pain of sexual abuse. Some young men do also, but we'll focus on women in this answer because they experience it more often.)

Let me explain the types of sexual abuse, how people are affected, and the help they need.

Anyone can be a victim of sexual abuse, and any sexual activity carried out in an inappropriate context is abusive. Sexual abuse can be defined broadly as "any sexual activity, verbal, visual, or physical, engaged in without consent, which may be emotionally or physically harmful and which exploits a person in order to meet another person's sexual or emotional needs. The person does not consent if he or she cannot reasonably choose to consent or refuse because of age, circumstances, level of understanding and dependency or relationship to the offender."[1]

There are several types of sexual abuse:

- *Verbal sexual abuse* consists of inappropriate words. This includes sexual jokes, sexual threats, comments about a person's body, solicitation, harassment, inappropriate sexual talk, and name-calling—any verbal expression with the purpose of belittling a person sexually.
- *Visual sexual abuse* includes voyeurism (staring at someone's body); exhibitionism (the displaying of pornographic material or genitals); and the showing of any sexual activity, such as masturbation or intercourse.
- *Physical sexual abuse* includes any inappropriate form of touching, from hugging to rape. Rubbing, holding, and kissing for the purpose of sexual gratification are examples.

Whether she has experienced sexual abuse once or a thousand times, every victim needs help to process her hurt, anger, confusion, and shame. Some victims are confused about whether they actually have been abused. Some people simply don't remember very stressful periods of their life. Memory blocks may be, but are not always, a symptom of abuse having occurred.

Some possible effects of sexual abuse include

Nightmares	Withdrawal
Pseudomaturity	Promiscuity
Low self-esteem	Fear of undressing
Outbursts of anger	Fear of being alone
Secrecy	Stomachaches
Insomnia	Memory blocks
Seductive behavior	Eating disorders
Self-hate	Depression
Suicidal feelings	Feelings of betrayal
Confusion of identity	Nervousness

These are a few of the possible effects sexual abuse can produce in children, women, and men. Not everyone who has these symptoms is a victim of sexual abuse, but people who wrestle with these symptoms need God's guidance for restoration, whatever the cause.

One of the most common emotions that sexual-abuse victims feel is rage. This intense anger, however, is not always focused on the perpetrator. That may be too threatening, so the victim often turns her venom on herself, on God, or on anybody else who may (knowingly or unknowingly) uncover her sense of shame.

Unresolved anger leads to resentment, bitterness, or retaliation. Anger or rage can—and often does—dominate the life of a sexual-abuse victim. Hatred gives her tremendous energy to prove she is a person who is valuable . . . or it destroys her motivation and hope, leaving her hopeless and depressed.

In his book *The Wounded Heart*, psychologist Dan Allender describes the faces of this rage:

> Contempt is complex and often hard to see. It sometimes masquerades as conviction; other times it seems like righteous indignation. At one point, it appears as a poor self-image, and at another, as a bad attitude toward others. Whatever its form or function, one thing can be assumed: *Contempt hinders the work of God.* It directs our sight away from our deepest longings and deflects the focus from our depravity and need for a Savior to an attack against our own or another's dignity.[2]

Sexual-abuse victims have difficulty with intimacy. They are afraid of feeling close to people because their need for closeness hasn't been met in a healthy way or with any consistency. Victims are afraid to trust because they might be betrayed again, but most are too lonely and afraid to be independent from other people. This paradox of emotions is overwhelming: They hunger for intimacy, but they are afraid of people.

Genuine intimacy requires the ability to make your own decisions, to talk about personal matters when and if you choose, to trust those who are trustworthy, and to form meaningful relationships with people.

Persons who have been sexually abused may

. . . be obsessed with romance.

. . . want someone to show affection, but then reject any affection that is offered.

. . . look for some magical quality in another person that will make them feel safe and complete.

. . . take themselves too seriously.

. . . use sex as a substitute for intimacy.

. . . be extremely critical of others and of themselves; they may interpret simple misunderstandings in a relationship as betrayal.

. . . be very suspicious and constantly test people to see if they are trustworthy.

. . . constantly seek intimacy with somebody—anybody; they may be desperate for intimacy but unable to be intimate.

The ability to trust has been crushed, especially in childhood incest. Girls who have been abused by a nonfamily member and who have a healthy family usually respond fairly quickly to help, but victims who come from disruptive and critical homes have a very difficult time learning to trust.

To make up for their inability to trust, some victims try to control their life by accumulating money or power and controlling other people. Others isolate themselves, rationalize, avoid people, run away, suspect all others, and evaluate virtually everything. Even when they fail, they keep on trying to control rather than risk trusting.

Dan Allender describes three specific ways abuse victims try to control themselves and their relationships. Some become "the good girl" and are very compliant, sweet, and gentle in the hope of winning approval and avoiding any conflict. Others become "the tough girl" and assume a defiant attitude in any and every relationship. They demand to be on top and in control so they won't be hurt again. And still others become "the party girl" and give in to the supposed pleasures of sexual escapades. They hope a multitude of sexual encounters will somehow meet their need for intimacy. All three of these relational styles are attempts to find some meaning in life, as well as to avoid more pain. But they fail to resolve the deep hurt and anger in their life.[3]

Victims of sexual abuse need loving, Christ-centered, consistent, regular counseling. At first the person needs to find at least one person (usually a counselor or a close friend) she can begin to open up to. Over time she can begin to trust a support group. In this powerful environment she will learn to be honest with God and pour out her hurt and anger to him. As time goes on, she will slowly rebuild the devastated parts of her life.

Encourage your friend to trust God and let him deliver her from all her fears and her need to control. She can learn to trust and find wholeness again.

Remembering this might help:

This is an explosive, difficult issue and too big a burden for you to carry alone.

NOTES

1. Cynthia A. Kubetin and James D. Mallory Jr., *Beyond the Darkness* (Houston, Tex.: Rapha, 1992), 3.
2. Dan B. Allender, *The Wounded Heart* (Colorado Springs, Colo.: NavPress, 1995), 88–89.
3. Ibid., 174–185.

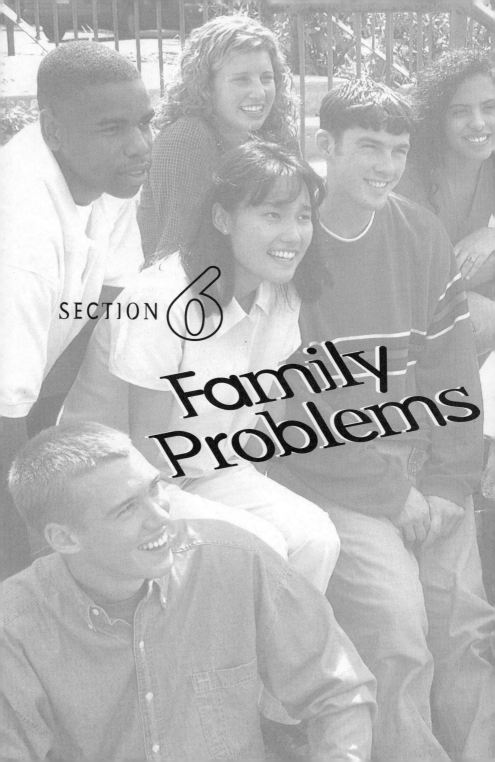

SECTION 6

Family
Problems

Hope for the American Student

When you feel as if nobody
cares and you need someone
to talk to, call the HOPELINE:
1-800-394-4673.

A caring encourager will be
on the line to offer you hope
from a biblical perspective
24 hours a day, 7 days a week,
365 days a year.

"Every adult fully aware . . .
every student receiving care!"

37

I can't stand my brother (or sister)! Is murder OK? (Not really!) How can we get along better?

GOSH, YOURS IS THE ONLY FAMILY in the world where the kids don't get along. (Not really!)

The point where you are now ("I can't stand . . .") didn't happen overnight. Slowly, gradually, over time, you and a sibling learned to despise each other. Is that too harsh a word? Maybe. Maybe not.

Some sibling rivalry is almost universal in families, but it doesn't have to destroy people. The normal competition occurs even in the healthiest of families. Kids want attention. They want a parent's affection, so they naturally compete for it with their brothers and sisters. This competition is a normal part of being human, but it can go beyond being normal when the members of a family are wounded by the effects of divorce, drugs, death, or disease. Deep family problems leave kids (parents, too) desperate for security and love. In these disturbed families the competition is far more intense because the stakes are higher and the needs are greater.

Before long, minor irritations become major rubs. Rolled eyes and a sigh escalate into a verbal bite. A slightly sarcastic remark becomes scathing ridicule. By then, the siblings have developed a destructive pattern of relating to each other. This habit took time to develop, and it will take time and effort to change.

Let me tell you five steps to take that will make this relationship better:

Step 1: Pray, asking God for wisdom to know how to change and for strength to do it. And I mean to change yourself, not your brother or sister. "What?" you ask. "Are you kidding? If that brat didn't act so stupid, we wouldn't have a problem!"

Maybe. But I've never seen sibling rivalry where only one person was at fault and the other person was blameless. As you pray, God will help you recognize your need to take responsibility for your own behavior. You can't change your brother or sister. You can only change yourself. One day you will stand before Christ to give an account of your words and behavior (1 Corinthians 3:10-15). When the celestial movie screen shows how you related to your brother or sister, you will want to hear Christ say, "Well done, my good and faithful servant. . . . Let's celebrate together!" (Matthew 25:21).

So the first step is to pray and make a commitment to respond in a way that honors the Lord. That commitment also involves forgiveness and repentance. Forgive your sibling for bugging the snot out of you, and repent of the times you've done your own share of bugging. Repentance is a decision to change your future behavior too. That's what the next steps cover.

Step 2: Stop nagging. Stop your very witty but very sarcastic remarks. Stop rolling your eyes when he says something stupid. And stop sighing every time she makes a remark.

Step 3: Look for good things in him or her, and verbalize them. It may be difficult at first, but keep looking until you can find a few things you appreciate about your brother or sister. And then (gulp!) speak them. That's right—out loud. And do it often. Not the same one every time! As you do this, you'll begin to notice more good, positive things about your brother or sister. You might start out by saying something like, "Your hair doesn't look quite as bad today as it usually does." But soon you'll graduate to, "Good job on your chemistry test!" Focus especially on character qualities, like integrity, honesty, kindness, and generosity. And speak of them often.

Step 4: Bite your lip! Oh, you'll still notice the revolting, disgusting, immature things your brother or sister does (even if you are years younger!), but don't go back to the same old patterns. If you blow it, apologize and keep going. A sincere apology will do wonders for a relationship. (Just ask my wife!)

Step 5: Take the initiative to be a friend. Do some fun things together. Offer to help with homework. Ask about his day. (When you ask, make sure it doesn't sound as if you're thinking, *Tell me what happened today so I can make fun of you!* That probably won't help build trust and friendship!) Tell her about your day without being asked. After a while, you may just find yourself enjoying the relationship. (No, I'm not delirious. I've actually seen this happen a time or two!)

As with any other changes God wants us to make, he doesn't expect us to do it alone. Talk to your youth pastor or someone else to get advice and encouragement. Ask that person to pray for you and to hold you accountable for how you respond in this relationship.

I know all this sounds impossible if you genuinely hate your brother or sister, but nothing is impossible with God! I hope God works and you learn to genuinely treasure that relationship!

I was the middle son in our family. When my little brother, Richard, was born, I moved into my older brother's room. When Richard was no longer a baby, my older brother, Denny, wanted a room by himself, so I moved in with Richard. When Denny moved away to go to college, I finally had the chance to get my own room. However, I chose not to have my own room because I didn't want to leave my little brother. Both of us enjoyed being together so much that we stayed in the same room even though the other bedroom was empty. To this day, Richard is my best male friend. We enjoy doing all kinds of things with each other, and we do things for each other that we wouldn't do for anybody else. He's younger, and he's uglier (I had to get that in!), but we have a great time.

One night Richard and I sneaked out the window. We loaded up our wagon with toilet paper and wrapped Mr. Williams's house. When we were through, we knocked on his door and began to run off, but Mr. Williams came to the door too quickly and saw us. We ran like crazy—and we left the wagon behind!

We ran home and told Denny that Mr. Williams would probably call Dad any minute. It was two-thirty in the morning. Sure enough, the phone rang, and Denny answered it as if he were Dad. He made his voice real deep, and he tried to sound just like Dad. Only one little problem: Dad walked in and listened to him!

Dad asked, "What's going on?"

The moment of truth (more or less) had arrived. Richard piped up, "Denny just wrapped Mr. Williams's house, and he's talking to him now." He pointed to Denny, and Denny was so cool.

Denny turned to Dad and said, "Yeah, I did it, Dad."

Dad made Richard and me go back to bed as he said to Denny, "You tell Mr. Williams you'll be right there to clean it up."

Denny nodded. "Yes, sir." And then he went down to Mr. Williams's house and cleaned up all the toilet paper. (We had done a really good job!) Denny had taken the heat, and he was really mad at us!

The next day Mr. Williams brought our wagon back to our house. He told Dad, "I appreciate Denny for cleaning up the mess, but it wasn't Denny who wrapped my house. It was Al and Richard." *Oooops!*

Dad, shall we say, applied the board of education to the seat of knowledge! And Denny died laughing.

Cool memory, huh? Yeah—that's what I have—cool memories of my siblings and me.

Remembering this might help:

You can't change your brother or sister. You can only change yourself. Ask God for wisdom to know how to change and for strength to do it.

38

I feel as if my parents hate me. What's the deal?

ALMOST ALL YOUNG PEOPLE HAVE big-time conflicts with their parents. For some it happens only very rarely, but for others it's an everyday thing. It hurts any time it happens.

There could be a number of reasons you feel the way you do.

1. *If there has been a lot of conflict between you and your parents and you know your attitude toward them has been wrong, you could be experiencing guilt.* These guilt feelings could cause you to assume some things that aren't true. You might feel you don't deserve your parents' love, or maybe you don't understand how they could really love someone like you. And you may have wrongly assumed that they don't love you at all.

2. *The anger they express may have nothing to do with you at all.* They may be furious at an ex-spouse, their employer, a trusted friend who betrayed them, some situation that is out of control, their finances, your brother or sister, or someone else. But for some reason they don't feel they can express their rage toward that person or situation. You are safer. And you are available. No, it's not fair! But expressing anger at someone when you are really angry at someone else happens all the time—maybe even with you!

3. *You may have blown it big-time!* Your parents may be very disappointed in your behavior, and they may have a hard time forgiving you.

4. *Your parents may have very high expectations for you— maybe way too high.* Some parents pressure their children to succeed because as grown-ups they want to feel good about themselves. Or maybe they do it because they don't want their kids to make the same mistakes they made when they were young. When expectations aren't met, people tend to get angry at the one who blocked their goals. And right now, that might be you! (I'm not saying that's right or fair. I'm just pointing out one of the reasons for anger.)

5. *If your parents are angry at you right now, it doesn't mean they don't love you.* Almost all parents love their children. The problem is that parents may not know how to show their love. And maybe we're wrong in saying they're angry. Maybe they're disappointed instead of angry. I know one man who has blown it over and over. He's been married several times, he has lived with women, and he's had children by several of them. He and his parents hardly speak anymore, even though his parents are raising one of his children. He thinks his parents hate him, but they don't. They are deeply disappointed in him.

Your parents may be having some problems that keep them from expressing their love. Let's look at a few:

- *Unless your parents have allowed God to do a major work of healing in their life, they may be parenting you exactly the way their parents raised them.* In other words, they are trying to control your behavior in the same way their parents tried to control theirs. If they grew up in a home where there was little affection or attention—no "I love you's" and no hugs—then they probably aren't very warm and affectionate toward you. If their parents were very critical and harsh, they may be just as tough on you. That's "normal" to them. On the other hand, some parents treat their kids in just the opposite way they were treated. If their parents were harsh, they may be too permissive. If their parents were absent, they may smother their kids with attention and control.

- *If your parents aren't Christians or if they aren't very strong in their faith, they probably don't understand true forgiveness.* It could be that you have hurt your parents in the past. Perhaps they were disappointed or embarrassed by something you did or said. Maybe they're angry because they feel rejected, unappreciated, taken advantage of, or not respected.

- *Perhaps your parents are experiencing bitterness.* Their lack of forgiveness can rapidly turn to bitterness if they don't deal with it. Unless your parents know how to forgive and how to apply forgiveness to your relationship, it will keep them from being able to show their love for you.

- *Your parents may not be showing love right now because of guilt.* It could be that they are feeling like failures as parents. When people feel guilty, they can admit they are guilty and change; but instead, many people get angry and defensive—in fact, that's what most people do.

- *Your parents may be fearful for you.* Perhaps they see some danger signals in your life. They realize that if these things don't change, you'll be headed for trouble. When they get panicky, that sometimes comes across as anger.

- *Perhaps there is a lot of pressure in your family right now.* A lot of teenagers don't realize how much pressure their parents are under. You need to cut them some slack. Your parents are trying to pay the bills, keep a job, make enough money to let you do some cool stuff, and maybe hassle with a boss who is irritating and unreasonable. On top of all this, they may be dealing with ex-spouse problems, aging parents, and other monumental things that make them edgy. I'm not saying it's OK for them to have a short fuse, but it is helpful to understand all the pressures they're under. You might ask them what pressures they face. After they recover from fainting, listen to what they have to say . . . and ask more questions so you really understand what's going on.

Whatever the reason, it sounds as if there's a communication problem in your home. It's important that you and your parents begin to listen to each other. Choose a time when things are calm at home, and ask your parents to talk about the issues in an unemotional way. Let them know you want a better relationship.

Some ground rules to set for the conversation: no yelling, no blaming, no storming out. Each person needs to be committed to listen until the person speaking is finished. Then others can ask questions to clarify things. A good way to make sure you understand each other is to reflect back what the person has just said: "Here's what I hear you saying. . . ." And use "I" statements: I feel. . . . I want. . . . I will. . . .

These are the most important qualities of a good communicator (parent or young person):

- A sense of warmth and respect for others
- A high degree of emotional security and stability
- An interest in others that allows alternative points of view
- A commitment to listen
- The ability to separate emotions from behavior
- A healthy sense of humor
- A sensitivity to the needs and interests of others[1]

Don't expect to get everything cleared up in one talk. Focus on the big problems (no more than two or three of them). If these get resolved, you can go on down the list in other conversations. Be realistic in your expectations. People will probably make mistakes and break the ground rules a time or two. When that happens, stop, remind each other of what you're trying to do, calm down, and then keep going. (You may need to take a break in the middle to cool off. That's OK. This isn't a speed drill!) And come back often to clear the air and work on understanding each other. It's worth it!

If this doesn't work, talk to a Christian counselor or pastor who can help. Don't let a hurtful situation keep getting worse.

Paul advises us: "Don't use foul or abusive language. Let everything you say be good and helpful, so that your words will be an encouragement to those who hear them" (Ephesians 4:29). Our families would be a lot different if we all applied this one verse, wouldn't they? Whether or not anybody else in the family is willing to make that commitment, make it yourself. Such a decision may not make your family change, but it will be sure to change you! And it will be a terrific habit to get into—one that will have a powerfully positive effect on every relationship for the rest of your life!

Remembering this might help:

It sounds as if there is a communication problem in your home. It's important that you and your parents begin to listen to each other.

NOTES

1. Adapted from William Lee Carter, *Family Communication* (Houston, Tex.: Rapha, 1992).

39

I've really hurt my parents. How can I make it right with them?

THREE CHEERS FOR YOU! You have shown an amazing level of maturity. You have faced your problem and accepted the responsibility for it. That's great! But please understand the seriousness of the sin of rebellion. You've sinned not only against your parents but also against God. The Bible says that "rebellion is as bad as the sin of witchcraft" (1 Samuel 15:23). That's serious! It also says children are to "obey" and "honor" their parents (Ephesians 6:1-3). That's God's command, not just his suggestion.

Here are three things you need to do to make things right:

1. *Confess your sin to God.* This means you agree with him that it is sin and you believe that he has already paid the price to forgive you. John wrote, "If we confess our sins to him, he is faithful and just to forgive us and to cleanse us from every wrong" (1 John 1:9). God's forgiveness is like a box of detergent that Jesus bought for you. Repentance and confession are like the water that activates that detergent and cleanses you from your sin. The box will never run out. You just need to know how to use it.

2. *Ask your parents to forgive you.* You need to be specific, humble, and sincere. They may or may not respond to

you properly. Some parents express their anger again, some feel guilty and withdraw, but many are thrilled that you would take responsibility and ask them to forgive you. Their response is up to them. You can do the right thing, letting God deal with your parents.

3. *Begin to make the changes needed in your life to be obedient to the Lord.* Talk is cheap. What your parents want to see (and what God wants to see also) is how you walk your talk. They don't expect perfection, but they want to see if you are sincere. Make yourself accountable to a mature Christian, such as your youth pastor or a godly uncle or aunt. This person can help you see areas in your life that need work and can give you steps to follow. Be sure to commit your relationship with your mom and dad to the Lord every day, asking him to help you understand your parents better and show you how to honor them.

All of us have conflicts with our parents from time to time. However, we can rest in God's promise that if our goal is to honor them, God will bless us richly!

One of the biggest sources of conflict between teenagers and parents is over independence. Parents want their teens to be safe and wise; young people want to make their own decisions about money, friends, use of their time, and every other issue in life. Those different goals produce conflict—sometimes a lot of it!

I know a girl who tried to resolve the conflict by lying to her parents. At first she stretched her lines only a little, such as when she told her parents she went to the lake with her best friend but didn't tell them about the two boys who went with them. Soon she began lying about all kinds of things.

She covered her stories for about a month, but her parents finally realized the stories were full of holes. When her mom and dad caught her in her web of deceit, they blew a fuse!

We can tell our parents the truth for years and years, but if we lie to them a few times, they stop trusting us. We have to prove ourselves all over again, which is hard on everybody. That doesn't mean the relationship is over. It just means we have to work hard to rebuild trust and good communication. If you've hurt your parents, take responsibility. Tell them those three little words, "I was wrong." And commit yourself to earning their trust again. It will take time, but it's worth it.

Here is something that might help. Ask your parents, "What can I do to earn your trust again?" Ask them to be specific. You see, it's not magic. It takes good, honest communication and hard work. Trust is rebuilt a brick at a time. So you'll need to be patient with yourself and with your parents. If you aren't making progress, ask your pastor or a good Christian counselor to step in and help you and your parents take these steps. There's nothing wrong with needing some help. That's what pastors and counselors do all the time!

The trust of your family may be shattered right now, and certainly you can't force them to take the steps that will rebuild the relationship. All you can do is be honest and take the steps *you* need to take. The rest is up to them and God.

Remembering this might help:

Commit yourself to earning your parents' trust again. It will take time, but it's worth it.

40

Should I obey my parents if they aren't Christians?

IN EPHESIANS 6:1-3 PAUL WRITES, "Children, obey your parents because you belong to the Lord, for this is the right thing to do. 'Honor your father and mother.' This is the first of the Ten Commandments that ends with a promise. And this is the promise: If you honor your father and mother, 'you will live a long life, full of blessing.'"

Some young people who don't want to obey these verses use the question above as a cop-out, but some have legitimate concerns. I've heard and seen a few teenagers (usually fairly new Christians) struggling against the desires of their parents. These kids want to be free! They want to make their own choices! But they still live at home and are still under the authority of their parents. These new believers find the verses in Ephesians 6 and say, "Hey, I 'belong to the Lord,' but my parents don't. So I don't have to do what they say anymore!" Wrong-o, rebellion breath!

In this passage Paul means for us to obey our parents as we would obey the Lord. Paul doesn't say, "Obey only Christian parents." He also doesn't say, "Obey your parents if they are right." He says to "obey your parents" (unconditionally) because it is the right thing to do.

An exception to this would be if your parents asked you to do something that was morally or legally wrong. It is God's job to hold your parents accountable, not yours. They will have to answer to him one day for all the decisions they have made. If your parents ask you to lie, steal, or cheat, you can explain to them that you can't do that because it is a sin that dishonors God . . . and could get you into serious trouble, too. I know of one teenager who refused to obey his parents when they asked him not to attend one of my concerts. He told them, "It's a Christian event, and God wants me to go!" Hey, I appreciate the sincerity, but going to a concert isn't a moral issue. If the parents told him he couldn't read or own a Bible, that's much more serious. Make sure you don't confuse a genuine moral or ethical issue with something that is far less significant.

Recently a student came to me and said, "Al, my parents are racists. I can't stand the way they talk about people who are different from them!" We may think we live in an enlightened age, but racism is still alive and well in the hearts of a lot of people. It is usually the product of ignorance and fear. Often people condemn those they don't understand and fear those who are different from them. Racism is unreasonable. In some people, it is more than just preferring their own kind; it is genuine hatred of others.

If your parents are like this, don't get caught up in their hatred. Be an individual. Walk with Christ, and love all of God's people, no matter what color their skin might be. Your careful reason and love can change lives—maybe not the racist's life, but at least yours. Study the Scriptures to see how Jesus treated Samaritans and Romans, or check out what Paul said in Ephesians 2:14 about breaking down "the wall of hostility" between Jews and Gentiles. But be careful around parents who are violent in their hatred. "Be as wary as snakes and harmless as doves" (Matthew 10:16). Go to your pastor or counselor to talk about your fears and what you can do to honor the Lord when you try to relate to your racist parents.

The command in Ephesians 6 distinguishes between obeying and honoring. It's clear that you are obligated to obey your parents as long as you are under their authority. That's what it means to be "a child" in Paul's passage. You are under their authority as long as you live in their house, eat their food, and accept their money for college and other expenses. You are no longer under their authority when you are on your own. At that point you are to be a functioning adult under the authority of a local body of believers, a church. (Some people believe young women are under the authority of their parents until they marry. At that point their husband becomes their authority.) Even when you are on your own, however, you are to honor your parents. You do that by showing respect, by not belittling them or being sarcastic, and by doing your best to demonstrate grace and truth to them. Paul said, "Do your part to live in peace with everyone, as much as possible" (Romans 12:18). "Everyone" especially includes your parents!

Certainly you will have more freedom—and responsibility—when you are on your own, but I want to caution you against the spirit of rebellion. If you can't wait to get away from your parents, that shows a real strain in the relationship. Pray, asking God for the grace to love and forgive; and seek to build a loving, understanding relationship between you and your parents. For some, this is easy. But for many others, the deep pains of abuse and abandonment make reconciliation difficult. It cannot happen without God's grace and power. Remember, all you can do is all you can do. You can't make somebody respond in love and trust. Your job involves these three things:

1. Take responsibility for your own behavior.
2. Choose to love no matter what the response.
3. Keep committing yourself to the Lord in the process.

The verses in Ephesians don't say that you are to honor your parents only if you feel they have earned it. Treat them with dignity and respect, and God will smile on you. Your parents are much more likely to come to Jesus if they see Jesus in you!

Remembering this might help:

You are obligated to obey your parents as long as you are under their authority. Even when you are on your own, you are to honor your parents by showing respect and by doing your best to demonstrate grace and truth to them.

41

How can I tell my parents about Jesus?

I TALK TO A LOT OF YOUNG MEN and women who have
come to Christ and who desperately want their parents
to experience his love and forgiveness. I love to see the
expressions on their faces and hear the love in their voices
as they talk about how much they long for their parents to
trust Christ.

Some of these young evangelists have gone home after
trusting Christ at a concert or camp, walked in the door, and
said something sensitive like, "Hey, Mom and Dad! You're
going to hell! Repent right now!" Man, that's a message
they'll remember!

A friend of mine who is a pastor tells young people to
"use few words and a big life" to share Christ with family
members. Actions speak louder than words to your family,
so it's important to live a life consistent with what you
believe. Your parents won't buy what you advertise if it
doesn't seem to work in your life.

Unbelieving parents are just like everyone else without
Jesus. They hurt, they have problems, they get confused, and
they're looking for answers. They need forgiveness and help.
If they don't see the love and peace of Jesus in your life, it is
going to be hard for them to believe he can do anything for
them.

That doesn't mean you have to be perfect. It means you know how to admit when you're wrong and ask for their forgiveness. Do your best to obey and honor your parents. When you're "walking your talk," God will provide opportunities for you to share your faith with your parents.

And don't forget to pray every day for your parents' salvation. Don't get too discouraged if they don't respond right away. I've talked to people who prayed for twenty or thirty years for their parents to respond to Christ, and finally, finally, they saw the fruit of their prayers. To be honest, I've also talked to a few people who prayed long, hard, and sincerely for parents who never responded. Our prayers don't force someone to respond. Parents have their own free will just as everyone else does, so they'll make their own choice. But our prayers can unleash God's power to bring people and circumstances into our parents' life that will encourage them to see "the glorious light of the Good News that is shining upon them" and "understand the message we preach about the glory of Christ, who is the exact likeness of God" (2 Corinthians 4:4). Then it's up to them.

Pray that God will help you live consistently for him. Pray that the Holy Spirit will use you, your friends, or someone else to show your parents their sinful nature and their need for Christ.

Remembering this might help:

Live a life consistent with what you believe. Then God will provide opportunities for you to share your faith with your parents.

42

My parents fight a lot. How can I help them get along and not get divorced?

MORE AND MORE YOUNG PEOPLE find themselves in this situation. Day after day they watch the relationship between their parents deteriorate. They want to stop the downward spiral of destruction, but they don't know how. Some parents explode in rage at each other, blaming, name-calling, yelling, and cursing. In other families the problem is not the explosions; it's the lack of them. Both parents avoid bringing up problems. They are furious and deeply hurt, but they sulk and withdraw, never communicating how they feel. In most strained marriages, there's one of each—one who explodes and one who passively takes it. Explosions and withdrawals have at least one thing in common: Neither of these responses resolves any of the problems.

It's great that you want to help, but be careful. It's primarily your parents' problem to work out, not yours. Sure, you're affected, but they have to be willing to take the steps to change and resolve the issues in their marriage. You are responsible *to* them, but not *for* them. Let me explain what I mean. Being responsible *for* someone means we try to control their behavior. For instance, a mother is responsible to keep her two-year- old out of the street. She's responsible for his safety. But it's not your responsibility to control your parents. That's their deal! You are responsible to speak the truth to them, to love them enough to confront them, to comfort them and understand them, but not to make them change. This is a very, very important distinction. If you feel you have to control them, it makes you the parent, not the child. That's not a good role for you!

Let me give you some suggestions for your appropriate role:

- *Pray.* Ask God to work his grace and power in their life, causing them to admit their hurts and their sins. Then they can experience God's great comfort and forgiveness. Too many people try to run on empty tanks. We all need God to fill us so we can relate to people in truth and love. And pray for yourself and your brothers and sisters. All of you need God's touch.

- *Sit down with your parents.* Tell them how their relationship is affecting them, you, and your brothers and sisters. They probably already know all that, but they might be denying how bad things really are. Hoping nobody notices doesn't make problems go away—for you or them!

- *Ask your parents to get help.* Suggest that they go see your pastor or a competent Christian counselor who is skilled in helping troubled marriages. If your parents refuse, point out the destructive consequences that are already happening in the family: bitterness, rage, depression, psychosomatic illnesses, addictions, etc.

- *Try not to take sides.* Sometimes it's easy to take one side against the other, but avoid that like the plague if you can! Taking sides will only create more hurt and anger, and then you'll be in the middle of it! But watch out: One of your parents (or both) may accuse you of taking sides even when you aren't. They may think their accusation will make you change and take their side. Don't do it. Tell them both that you are trying to be neutral and objective and that you intend to speak the truth to both of them.

- *Get help for yourself.* Most young people in this situation are so focused on their parents' needs that they don't notice the deep hurt, confusion, and anger in their own life. You need help too! Talk to your youth pastor, a godly aunt or uncle, or some other mature Christian about what's going on. You'll need to cry and to grieve the feelings of hurt and hopelessness. Don't let yourself be a casualty of your parents' war.

- *Find some fun.* Don't become so focused on your parents' problems that you become too serious, depressed, and sullen. Make sure you do some fun things to keep your sanity (or what's left of it). Go to the mall with friends, get involved in sports, go fishing or hunting—do whatever is fun for you.

- *Don't give up.* I've seen young people try to help their parents stay together, but eventually the parents file for divorce anyway. In some cases, that leads first to a temporary separation, which often is the best thing that can happen to a relationship! In fact, a Christian psychologist, Norm Wright, suggests that couples who are considering divorce separate for a few months and attend divorce-recovery groups. That gives them an opportunity to see what it's really like to split up for good. In many, many cases, parents discover that the grass really isn't greener on the other side of the fence! Then they are willing to work on the problems that lasted so long and caused so many hurts.

But some couples choose divorce no matter what their children, friends, counselors, and pastors do to help them. Remember, they are the parents, the adults. They—not you—are responsible for their decisions. Love them and speak the truth to them. Be grateful when and if they make good choices; grieve when they don't, and get some help for yourself in the process.

When I was eleven my parents had a big fight, and it scared me to death. Somehow, I thought it was my fault. I was afraid my dad would walk out and never come back, so I stood at the front door to make sure he couldn't leave. Sure enough, he came toward the door, and I blocked him. He said, "Al, what are you doing? Move over, and let me out."

I pushed the door shut and cried, "You aren't leaving, Dad. I'm not letting you go." Tears streamed down my face as I pleaded and held the door shut. I wailed, "Dad, please don't go! Please don't leave us!"

He shook his head and said, "Son, I'm just going to the store to get some milk."

"Oh." I moved over and let him go.

I'm not relating this to be funny. This story is about the fears we feel when our parents fight and we feel out of control. Standing at the door was an expression of the depth of my fear that my family was breaking up. I didn't want that to happen. I couldn't let that happen!

That night Richard and I crawled down the hall to listen at Mom and Dad's bedroom door. (We did that pretty often.) That night we heard them say, "We can't fight in front of the children anymore. It's tearing them up." I think my fears and my pleading with my dad had a big impact on our family.

Remembering this might help:

You are responsible to speak the truth to your parents, to love them enough to confront them, to comfort them and understand them, but not to control them.

43

My parents are divorced and are always fighting. They try to use me to get back at each other. What can I do?

DIVORCE IS A HORRIBLE THING. God says, "I hate divorce!" (Malachi 2:16). Seldom does anything good come from divorce, regardless of how many problems there were in the marriage.

When spouses don't part as friends, the results are often devastating to the children. Bitterness toward an ex-husband or ex-wife can blind a parent to what he is doing to a child. Your parents are not deliberately trying to hurt you. They have been so badly hurt themselves that they can't see the pain they are causing you. Parents who want desperately to be supported may force the children to take sides against the ex. If they are successful, they feel better about themselves, and they have been able to exert a measure of revenge on the one who hurt them. Revenge is a powerful motivator, but it destroys everybody it touches.

Sometimes divorced parents blame their children and take their anger out on them, but some divorced parents react in the opposite way: They spoil their kids. They feel guilty for the family's breaking up, so they overcompensate by letting the children have anything they want, anytime they want it, no matter what the cost. Shrewd kids figure this out and may contribute to the problem by saying things like, "If you loved me, you'd give me _____" (fill in the blank).

These permissive parents don't give normal, healthy correction and discipline, so the child takes control of the relationship. Spoiling a child is just as damaging as blaming. It is motivated by guilt and fear, and it leaves the child without a clear sense of right and wrong. This type of relationship is passed down to the next generation when the child grows up and has a family.

The best way to put the brakes on parents' destructive actions is to confront your parents with the truth. Do this in love, not anger, and do it honestly. If you aren't strong enough to do this alone, ask your pastor, youth minister, or some other adult your parents respect to help you. Have both parents in the same room together. The adult you choose can help you explain your feelings and desires and can be a "referee" for your parents if necessary.

I suggest that all of you clearly define ground rules in the relationships. Write these down, and make sure each person has a copy. The ground rules might include the following:

- Each parent will agree not to use the children against the other parent.
- The children should speak out when they feel used for that purpose.
- Each person will refrain from gossip about others.
- There will be weekly or monthly progress reports from each person to be sure the relationships are progressing.
- Expectations about time spent together, vacations, gifts, and other points of contention will be worked out ahead of time and communicated clearly, perhaps with the help of the referee.

When you feel used as a tool to pit one parent against the other, speak the truth about how you feel and what's going on. Your referee may have to get involved several times to help work things out.

Remind yourself that your parents' divorce is not your fault. In spite of that, you probably have a lot of hurt and anger as a result of their decision to split up. Your youth pastor, an aunt or uncle, or a Christian counselor can help you work through your anger. Don't carry all that hurt in your heart alone.

Remembering this might help:

The best way to put the brakes on parents' destructive actions is to confront your parents with the truth. Do this in love, not anger, and do it honestly.

44

I have a blended family, and sometimes it's a real mess! What can I do?

AND WHAT EXACTLY DID YOU EXPECT? A picnic? Let's be honest. (And it's not as if I've been lying on every page up to now!) Blended families are combinations of lots of wounded people. Parents' first marriages ended either in divorce or in the death of a spouse. The whole family may have lived in fear and insecurity for years as they suffered through the deceased parent's illness or the bitterness of the marriage before the divorce. Often, single parents marry again before they have resolved the pain of the previous relationship. That complicates the new marriage, and an even higher percentage of second marriages end in divorce.

So where does that leave you? Probably in a family where the parents have unresolved wounds from a previous marriage. And they may have been married several times before— with unresolved hurts from each of those relationships! In addition to all of that, the children are thrown together without exactly *choosing* to be together! Normal sibling rivalry is now compounded by competition for attention and affection. This competition is related to the fact that there is a new stepparent (someone you may not trust). It is related to the way you feel about the parent you live with (someone you may be angry with for marrying that person you don't trust). It may also be related to your feelings about the other parent (who abandoned you in death or divorce). Normal sibling rivalry is now multiplied by ten to the thirty-seventh!

Here are some suggestions to help you in this mess:

- *Be realistic.* If you take a good, hard, objective look at the situation, what do you expect? Right! Problems, misunderstanding, miscommunication. One of our biggest problems is when our expectations are far too high and we hope to get far more attention and affection than we actually get.

- *Know your limits.* Lots of people around you have problems, but you aren't the Savior of the world. That job's already taken! You are responsible to speak the truth, communicate love, and take care of your business at home and at school. If other people in the family are acting weird, you can offer to help, but it's not up to you to control them.

- *Grieve your own hurts.* We usually think of grieving a death, but grief is appropriate in any loss. Losing the security of a stable home, losing a parent, and losing a part of your identity in the process have undoubtedly hurt you a lot. Take time to feel the sadness. Learn to cry and express your hurt. Grief takes time and attention; if you don't allow for it, the sense of loss will eat you alive from the inside out.

- *Forgive.* People in blended families almost always have a lot of wounds. They feel misunderstood, betrayed, and abandoned. Bitterness robs us of the joy of life. We may think that harboring resentment hurts the person we are angry with, but it's really us that it hurts. We need to forgive, but we can't forgive those who have

hurt us if we don't feel forgiven for our own sins.
Paul wrote to the Colossian believers, "You must make
allowance for each other's faults and forgive the person
who offends you. Remember, the Lord forgave you,
so you must forgive others" (Colossians 3:13). As you
experience forgiveness, you will be more willing and
able to extend it to others who have hurt you.

- *Heal.* A broken leg takes medical care, a cast, and months
  to mend the bone. After the cast is removed, physical
  therapy may take a couple of months more to strengthen
  the muscles. It's the same with emotional healing. These
  wounds require time, attention, hard work, and patience
  for the damage to be repaired.
- *Have fun.* Find some things that you really enjoy doing
  (and that are relatively harmless!), and have some fun.
  Some of these activities might be with people in the
  blended family, but some will be with your friends or by
  yourself. We all need a hobby and some laughs, especially
  if we are in stressful situations.
- *Be filled with grace, and speak the truth.* The apostle
  John said that Jesus was "full of grace and truth" (John
  1:14, NIV). As you walk with him, you will be filled with
  his grace (kindness, forgiveness, gentleness, and love).
  And you will be able to communicate truth (about God,
  your situation, your feelings, and the consequences of
  others' behavior). The transition in your attitudes and
  behavior occurs as the Holy Spirit changes your perspective
  and motivation and as you make the difficult choices to
  honor Christ in every conversation and situation.
- *Develop friendships.* A blended family sometimes experiences a honeymoon period when it begins, but soon the
  hurts, unfulfilled expectations, and misunderstandings can

take their toll. Don't let bitterness, withdrawal, and accusations become a habit in your relationships. Work on developing friendships with as many people as possible, including those in your blended family. And take the initiative to be a friend first.

Remembering this might help:

Be realistic in your expectations for attention and affection; grieve your losses; forgive; allow time for emotional healing; take the initiative to be a friend.

45

My brother (or sister) is smoking dope. Should I tell our parents?

SMOKING DOPE. DRINKING. Doing drugs. Sniffing glue. Lying. Cheating. Having sex.

When you see someone you love heading down the wrong path, it breaks your heart. Love demands that you take action, but it also requires that you be wise as you determine the specific steps to take.

In writing to the Galatians, Paul instructed them, "If someone is caught in a sin, you who are spiritual should restore him gently. But watch yourself, or you also may be tempted. Carry each other's burdens, and in this way you will fulfill the law of Christ" (Galatians 6:1-2, NIV). What "law of Christ" is Paul talking about? It's the second of the two great commandments: "Love your neighbor as yourself" (Matthew 22:39).

Notice some things Paul says. You are to act if you see the person "caught in a sin." Some of us want to confront people for things they do that bug us but aren't sins at all—like having a bad haircut or chomping on ice! That's not what Paul is referring to. He's talking about *sins*—things that cause heartache to people and dishonor to God.

Paul says to help the person "gently," not blast his head off! Our goal is to restore the person to wholeness and right living, not to render judgment and revenge.

He also warns us to "watch" ourselves or we "may be

tempted." Tempted to do what? To drink or smoke or lie? Maybe. Maybe not. I think Paul is talking about the temptation to think we're better than other people because we don't engage in the same gross sins they do. Pride is just as destructive. So Paul wants us to be careful not to be boastful or haughty but to be humble as we confront the person. Our attitude should be "there but for the grace of God go I."

OK, so what do you actually do when your brother or sister is messing up big-time? Should you squeal? This is what I recommend:

1. **Confront your sibling privately, and describe the activities you've seen.** Giving an eyewitness account is much more powerful than repeating what others have told you, but that may be all you have to go on. Your brother (or sister) may say you're wrong . . . or you misunderstood. He may claim it's no big deal. He may even say he's prayed about it and God told him it was OK. Solomon had a word for people like this. He wrote, "There is a path before each person that seems right, but it ends in death" (Proverbs 14:12). Ask your brother to stop his sinful behavior and get some help. Tell him what damages you already see in his life and the damage you foresee if he doesn't stop. Plead with him to change.

If he stops, great! Praise God! If he doesn't . . .

2. **Confront your sibling again.** This time warn him that if he does it again—even one more time—you're going to tell Mom and Dad. The reason you're going to tell them, you explain to him, is that you care about him too much to stay quiet. Be strong: Tell him this isn't a threat; it's a promise! And you're doing it for his own good.

What do you expect during this confrontation? Maybe your

brother will say, "Oh, thank you so much for caring! I'll be happy to stop right now." Probably not! In most cases, the person either lashes out at the one confronting him, or he weeps and pleads for understanding. Both of these (the anger and the weeping) can be ways to manipulate you to back off. One is designed to intimidate. The other tries to play on your sympathies. Don't back off. Be kind, but be strong and resolute. You can tell if his weeping is because he is broken-hearted before God or if he's just using the tears to jerk your chain and get you to leave him alone. If he is willing to confess his sin and repent, then it's real. If he wants you to keep quiet about it and not bring it up again, then it probably isn't.

If he changes, great! If not . . .

3. **Tell your parents.** And be sure to let your sibling know that you told them. He may yell and accuse you of betraying him, but be strong. Tell him that you promised you were going to tell them if he continued. And you did it because you love him.

It is a good idea to be with your parents when they confront him about his behavior. No, you're not going just for the excitement. You need to be there to be sure he doesn't twist your words and squirm out of the situation. He probably has lied to your parents plenty of times to cover up his behavior. He may be a master at it! You need to be there to tell what you've seen and how you confronted him a time or two before.

Now, here's a tough one. Your parents may not like confrontation any more than you and your brother do. They may want to "sweep it under the rug." Your dad may say, "Well, boys will be boys." Your mother may say, "I'm sure he won't ever do it again." Their goal may be just to get the confrontation over with. On the other hand, one or both of your parents might go ballistic! If you fear one of these extreme responses, be sure to have a talk with them ahead of time and communicate your fears and hopes for their confrontation.

Remember, your responsibility is simply to obey the Lord and do the right and loving thing. You can't make your brother repent or your parents respond correctly. That's their deal.

One more thing: Your brother's behavior might come from any number of causes. Unless that cause is uncovered and resolved, he is very likely to go back to the same destructive behavior—or maybe a different one—before long. Help your parents and your brother look underneath and find the cause. It might be an excessive interest in experimentation, a habit of hanging with the wrong crowd, the need to escape deep hurts, or the need for intimacy. (If it is hidden hurts, it's possible that other members of the family may need some help in this area also.)

Take a look at yourself in this process. It is a very stressful thing to care enough to confront someone you love. You may be filled with pride one minute and devastated the next. Get some help for yourself along the way. You'll need it!

Remembering this might help:

Confront your brother or sister privately. If your sibling doesn't stop, confront him again with a promise to tell Mom and Dad. If he still doesn't change, tell your parents.

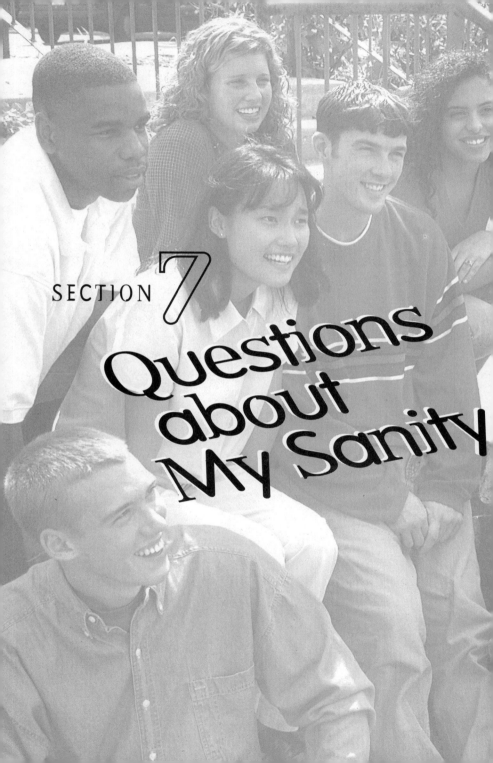

SECTION 7

Questions about My Sanity

Hope for the American Student

When you feel as if nobody cares and you need someone to talk to, call the HOPELINE: 1-800-394-4673.

A caring encourager will be on the line to offer you hope from a biblical perspective 24 hours a day, 7 days a week, 365 days a year.

"Every adult fully aware . . . every student receiving care!"

46

I feel so guilty all the time! What will give me some relief?

I'VE RELIVED THE PLANE CRASH in my mind a million times. A friend lost his life that day. I honestly don't think I did anything wrong, but I still feel guilty. Maybe I could have prevented it somehow. I know my feelings aren't reasonable, but I have them anyway. I've asked myself—and I've asked God—why that crash happened, but I still don't have any answers. I probably won't have any until I see Jesus face-to-face.

Many of us feel guilty. We feel guilty about what we've done and haven't done. We feel guilty about what we've said and haven't said, felt and haven't felt. We feel guilty about almost everything. This kind of guilt produces feelings of worthlessness and shame.

The guilt and shame that I'm referring to are not the kind that lead to an objective judgment of your offense. If you have been caught going eighty-five miles per hour on the highway and the judge pronounces, "Guilty as charged," that is objective guilt. In that sense, all people stand before God as guilty and in need of the forgiveness and acceptance of the Cross. But the guilt that we are looking at here is a different kind. It is the painful, gnawing perception that we are worthless, unacceptable, and incapable of ever doing enough to be acceptable, no matter how hard we try.

There is a vast difference between these two kinds of guilt. One produces a sorrow that leads to positive, refreshing change. The other leads to a sorrow that only crushes. The apostle Paul described positive and negative guilt in his second letter to the Corinthian believers: "Now I am glad I sent [that letter], not because it hurt you, but because the pain caused you to have remorse and change your ways. It was the kind of sorrow God wants his people to have, so you were not harmed by us in any way. For God can use sorrow in our lives to help us turn away from sin and seek salvation. We will never regret that kind of sorrow. But sorrow without repentance is the kind that results in death" (2 Corinthians 7:9-10).

The realization of personal wrong, coupled with a knowledge of forgiveness, brings hope and change. However, the realization of personal wrong without that forgiveness brings bitter pangs of condemnation and hopelessness. In dysfunctional families, personal wrongs are magnified, while forgiveness, love, and acceptance are withheld. Those bitter pangs of condemnation are a way of life for the guilt-ridden person.

Guilt without forgiveness crushes a person. It crushes his dreams, his desires, and his personality. I know a young lady in high school who was driving a car that was hit when another car ran a red light. A passenger in her car, her best friend, was killed. It wasn't in any way this girl's fault, but she can't get over feeling that she is somehow to blame. She runs through *what if's* a million times a day in her mind. What if she had taken a different route? What if she had been just a little more careful? What if she had done something completely different that day? She is consumed with guilt over this tragic accident. And I wonder how oppressive her guilt would be if she were *really* responsible for her friend's death. Man, she would be in a coma!

All of us have done things that are wrong, but a guilt-ridden person attaches greater weight to those wrongs than he does to forgiveness. He is deeply ashamed, feeling that at least some of those terrible things he has done cannot possibly be forgiven.

Let's think more in-depth now about our feelings of self-worth. If these feelings come only from the things we do for others, then we can't say no to anything or anyone. If we do say no, we feel guilty. Even if we say yes and fail, we feel guilty. If we say yes and succeed but others don't appreciate us, our worth is shattered and we still feel guilty. Even success and praise bring only short-term relief. There is always the nagging fear of losing that approval. To please people, we take on their dreams and desires—not our own—and lose our personality in the process.

Anger compounds the guilt and reinforces our tragic sense of worthlessness. One young woman explained how she was pushed to the limit to help her boyfriend, who had a drinking problem. She got really mad at him but then thought, *He can't help it. If I were the kind of friend he needed, he'd be OK. It's all my fault!* She was infuriated again, but this time at herself for getting angry with her "poor, helpless" boyfriend. She called herself degrading and vile names. She punished herself for being so selfish and callous.

The crushing effects of guilt, shame, worthlessness, self-hatred, and self-condemnation take a heavy toll. Some people escape into a shell of numbness, passivity, or depression. Some develop psychosomatic illnesses. Others just plod along, day after day, year after year, under the oppressive weight of guilt. There are varieties of results, but only one cause: the crushing nature of guilt.

When we are motivated by guilt, it is usually related to a desire to avoid condemnation and to perform or measure up to certain standards. These standards may have been set by someone else or ourselves. We perform with a sense of urgency and desperation because we think we *have to*, not because we *want to*. Our motivation is characterized by *I have to* and *I can't* statements:

- I have to accomplish this today.
- I have to go here.
- I have to help this person in this way at this time.
- I have to say yes.
- I have to control my anger and hurt.
- I can't fail in this assignment.
- I can't let her down.
- I can't let my anger get out of control.
- I can't say no.

The capacity to say no, to make our own decisions, to relax, and to enjoy life is foreign to some of us because it doesn't contribute to our consuming goal in life: getting ahead, earning approval, and proving our worth.

Those who are oppressed by guilt live by *shoulds* and *oughts*, not by the confidence of feeling secure and significant. They are driven to have more, to be more, to say more, and to do more. The carrot dangles from the stick, always just out of reach. No matter how much they do, no matter how much they have, no matter how clever or successful they are, they almost always have the nagging thought that they should have done more, said something else, or been better.

Unfortunately, the law of sowing and reaping takes effect in the area of guilt just as it does in every other part of life. If guilt has been used to motivate and manipulate you, then you will probably use it on others. It is a strange fact that even if you detest the way you have been treated, this model is so strong that you may find yourself treating others the same way.

A young man realized that he viciously condemned his girlfriend and withdrew his affection from her to manipulate her. He felt terrible about it. He loathed and despised himself when he did it, but this was how his parents had treated him. It was the only way he knew to act, even though he realized it was wrong and knew how much it hurt her.

The ingredients that are used to manipulate us are the same ones we tend to use with others. We speak the same words of praise and condemnation. We use the same actions, tone of voice, and expressions. We express the same aggressive, angry behavior. Or we exhibit the same withdrawal and passivity. On the other end of the spectrum, instead of harshly condemning, we may withdraw; instead of being passive and neglectful, we may smother. A poor model will usually produce a poor offspring who will be out of balance either as a duplicate or an opposite.

But there is hope! You can overcome oppressive guilt by learning to focus on the unconditional love and forgiveness of Christ. His love is powerful, and he is worthy of our intense zeal to obey and honor him.

Although the Holy Spirit convicts both believers and

unbelievers of sin (John 16:8), his conviction of believers is not intended to produce pangs of guilt. Our status and self-worth are secure by the grace of God, and we are no longer guilty. Conviction deals with our behavior, not our status before God. Conviction is the Holy Spirit's way of showing the error of our performance in light of God's holy standard and truth. The Spirit's motivation is love, correction, and protection.

We need to affirm that Christ has forgiven us and has made us judicially righteous before God. Our sin does not result in condemnation. However, sin is harmful and brings dishonor to God. So we can confess our sin to God, claim the forgiveness we already have in Christ, and then move on in joy and freedom to honor him.

We may not experience joy and freedom immediately, especially if we have developed the painful habit of prolonged self-condemnation as a way of dealing with sin. Loving friends who listen to us and encourage us can be an example of God's forgiveness to us. As we become more honest about our feelings through these affirming relationships, we will be able to increasingly experience the freedom, forgiveness, and freshness of God's grace.

Remembering this might help:

Focus on the unconditional love and forgiveness of Christ.

NOTES

1. Except for personal anecdotes, the material in this chapter is adapted by permission from Pat Springle's *Co-dependency: A Christian Perspective* (Houston, Tex.: Rapha, 1990).

47

Sometimes I think it would be easier to just kill myself. What can I do to feel better and have some hope?

WHEN I WAS IN SEVENTH GRADE, our youth group went camping. I wanted to be really cool—like all seventh graders do. A new kid came along (I'll call him Randy) who really didn't fit in at all. Guess whose tent they put him in? Yep, mine. The other guys and I were having a great time doing the stupid things seventh-grade boys do. (Use your imagination, but not too much!) Randy, though, just sat alone in the corner of the tent. He didn't fit in. He didn't want to fit in.

We went to sleep late that night after pulling pranks and talking about all kinds of things. When we woke up the next morning, Randy was gone. The counselors got everybody together, and we looked all over for him. We found him in the lake. He had drowned.

I don't know if Randy wandered away in the middle of the night and fell in the water or if he killed himself, but we felt terrible. We wondered if we could have done something. We wondered if it was somehow our fault. It's a pretty heavy thing for a kid like Randy to die. That's a pretty heavy guilt trip for seventh graders like those of us who were left behind.

Lost. Alone. Helpless. Hopeless.

These are hard, stressful times we live in, aren't they? Families are breaking up; money is tight; there is so much violence and war. Drugs and alcohol are everywhere, and parents seem to have little time to show that they care. Friends betray us. Sometimes thoughts of suicide come from feelings of hopelessness. The idea of running away from our pain sounds good.

Many people have thoughts of "ending it all" when they experience devastating setbacks. Those fleeting thoughts are yellow flags telling us to pay attention to the pain inside and get some perspective and encouragement. A more serious signal, a red flag, is when a person has a specific plan for how to die. And a neon red flag waves when the person has the tools on hand to get the job done: a gun, a rope, pills, or whatever.

Maybe you are angry at your parents. You just want to get back at them and hurt them the way they have hurt you. Or maybe you are feeling angry at yourself and feel a desperate need to punish yourself because of something awful you've done. It could be that someone very close to you died, and you have an urge to join him or her. Your risk is greater if you have experienced

- recent suicide attempts
- addiction to alcohol or drugs
- uncontrollable rage
- painful, devastating losses
- adverse reactions to medications
- severe anxiety or depression

Whatever the reason, there is a battle going on inside you . . . and you need help to win the war. Well, there's hope! Jesus Christ offers not just eternal life in heaven but an abundant life now. You can have peace, love, joy, hope—everything you need. Jesus really loves you and understands your pain. He has the answers you need for all your problems. The answers may not be simple and easy, but they are strong and lasting.

Suicide is never the right answer. It is the taking of a precious, God-given life. It is sin. Some of us get so down that we've completely lost hope. We can't see any way out—or any way up. But there's always a way, a better way. You may not be able to see it now, but believe me, God has something wonderful and meaningful for every one of us, no matter how bleak things look.

The first step is to be honest about your pain and to get some help. Suicide is not a solution. You want relief from a bad situation and the pain you are experiencing. The relief will come with the help of a godly, Christian counselor. Please, immediately tell someone you trust—your pastor, youth leader, or another caring adult. Let this person help you find the answers God has for you. God's way is always best.

In Isaiah 61:3 God promises, "To all who mourn in Israel, he will give beauty for ashes, joy instead of mourning, praise instead of despair. For the Lord has planted them like strong and graceful oaks for his own glory." God will do this for you if you let him and if you do things his way.

You must not take matters into your own hands and play God. You must make a choice to reject the suicidal thoughts you are having and instead look to Jesus for help.

We all want to know that someone loves and cares for us. Jesus is that someone. He died for you so that you can live.

Remembering this might help:

Let a godly, caring adult show you how to receive from God "joy instead of mourning, praise instead of despair."

48

I feel really down. Hopeless. Out of control. What can I do?

WHEN TRACIE'S GRANDMA WAS DYING of cancer, it was tough watching Tracie hurt. I felt so helpless. I wanted to change things somehow. I wanted to make it different. But I couldn't. That was a really low point for me.

Another low point lasted a lot longer. After the plane crash my friend was dead, but I was alive. I was scared like crazy, but I was alive. I experienced what people call "survivor's guilt." I was glad to be alive, but I felt so guilty that I hadn't died too. I hated the fact that my buddy was gone. Why was I spared? Did I somehow cause his death? How could I keep on living? I felt really low . . . for a long, long time.

Another time I felt really depressed for a long time was when a brother in Christ lied to me. We were friends, close friends. I never dreamed he would betray me the way he did, and I never dreamed we would be unable to make it right between us. I tried to work it out. He only blamed me more. Finally I gave up. I closed up and went into a shell. I said, "I can't deal with this. It hurts too much."

If we live long enough, statistics show that most of us have been or will be depressed at some time in our life. It happens even though we all try to avoid it.

Hopelessness, helplessness, a sense of doom, and self-hatred are common symptoms of depression. In more severe forms, called "clinical depression," constant fatigue and either too much or too little sleep are common. The causes of depression can be physical (such as a tumor or the flu), but the most common cause is repressed anger.

Most of us experience periods of depression that are relatively mild. In fact, many people who feel this way don't even notice, much less admit, being depressed. They may appear to be grumpier than usual, experience a temporary change in eating or sleeping habits, withdraw from people, or not care about things they usually enjoy. Periods of depression often begin with some sort of loss—perhaps the loss of a relationship or a dream.

Moderate and severe forms of depression are harder to ignore. These more serious states of depression may occur because support is unavailable. Many families are not honest about painful emotions. Instead of experiencing comfort, love, and understanding, people in these families suppress their hurt and anger. When these feelings are "stuffed" for months or years, depression and outbursts of anger can occur.

While the most common cause of depression is internalized anger, depression is not the result only of stuffed feelings of anger. Some women suffer from severe, premenstrual depression in which mood swings, anger, and suicidal thoughts are common. Genetic factors may also play a role in making it likely that people will experience depression, particularly in the more severe types of depression. This means that if a person's family history includes severe depression, he may be prone to similar problems.

Severe depression may include

- weight loss or gain
- too little or too much sleep

- noticeable agitation or slowed functioning
- fatigue and loss of energy; feelings of worthlessness and guilt
- problems in concentrating and making decisions
- suicidal thoughts or plans

Certain kinds of depression may appear to be just the opposite of what you might expect. In "bipolar depressions" people are sometimes very down, but at other times they are up and excited or excessively irritable. In the manic (up) phase, the person may experience several of these symptoms: inflated self-esteem or a belief that he can do almost anything; a decreased need for sleep; a tendency to monopolize conversations; difficulty in organizing racing thoughts; distractibility; increased activity; and addictive behaviors such as drinking, overeating, and using drugs. Symptoms of a manic phase may interfere markedly with school or work, social activities, and important relationships. Somebody who is experiencing a mild manic state can be charming and productive, but when the disorder increases in severity, friends and family members suffer as well. In severe cases a person may experience delusional thinking or hallucinations and lose touch with reality.

I know several people who are bipolar. Sometimes they are the life of the party. They are excited and upbeat, and they accomplish all kinds of things. But now and then they go off the deep end. They withdraw into deep depression. I don't see them for days—even weeks. It's hard on me as a friend. I wonder how their family members live with these incredible ups and downs. I know that medication sometimes helps level out these episodes. I'm glad the Lord has provided these medicines so people can live as normally as possible.

Without medication, depressed people may feel angry, anxious, arrogant, bitter, bored, confused, cynical, fearful, guilty, shameful, hopeless, and helpless. They try to limit or stop their feelings of depression, but usually their efforts actually make them worse. For example, a person may buy something new to feel better. If she has the resources to do that, it may not cause a problem; but if she spends too much and gets into debt, then her depression may return with even greater intensity. Sometimes people use alcohol, drugs, tobacco, food, sex, television, the telephone, money, or any other substance, object, or person in an attempt to feel better.

If you know someone who has experienced any of these symptoms, here are some things you should know:

1. It's important to give others freedom to experience their own feelings. Don't try to talk them out of those feelings. Try to understand, not change, how they feel.
2. Anyone who really is beginning to deal with loss is likely to feel down and discouraged. It's normal, and it's part of the healing process.
3. Although depressed people may have experienced severe losses in the past, they need to know that others care about them now.
4. Bad feelings themselves don't hurt people, but the actions they may take to avoid those feelings might hurt them.

If you have experienced any symptoms of depression, talk to someone about your feelings. Find someone who will listen and care, whether it's a family member, a friend from church, a youth leader, or a school counselor. Ask that person to pray with you and for you. Don't keep your feelings to yourself.

Talking them through with someone will help you deal with those feelings. Depression is a serious problem that needs the power of God, the comfort of his people, and the life-changing truth of his Word to give hope and help.

Remembering this might help:

Talk to someone about your feelings. Don't try to keep them to yourself.

NOTES
1. Except for personal anecdotes, the material in this chapter is adapted from the booklet by Steve Spotts, *Depression* (Houston, Tex.: Rapha, 1992).

49

I think about being thin (or buff) all the time. Is there something wrong with me?

SO . . . YOU LOOK AT THE MODELS in the magazines or the actors and actresses on the screen. Then you look in the mirror, and you don't like what you see. That's a real shock! The truth is that only a very small number of people in the world are fabulously beautiful or handsome. If we compare ourselves to them, 99 percent of us are going to come up short.

But comparison is very common among young men and women. If you're a teenager, your body is changing, growing, and developing, so it's normal to notice what's going on with your shape. Comparing yourself to others is also normal—to a degree. You'll get into trouble, though, if you compare too much and if you compare yourself only to the most gorgeous people in the world. Not every girl can look like Vanessa Williams or Elle McPherson. Not every guy can look like me. (Ha!)

We cross over the line into unhealthy and sinful habits when we

> . . . **think about food all of the time.** When you have some time to relax and you can only think about how to eat so you'll look slimmer or stronger, that's out of bounds. *Anorexia nervosa* and *bulimia* are two very serious eating disorders.

Anorexics eat as little as possible. They are as thin as spaghetti; but when they look in the mirror, their eyes see a fat person! I know one young woman who ate a carrot and two leaves of lettuce a day, and she ran three to five miles almost every single day. Anorexia is a very serious health problem. People with this condition can (and do) die if they don't get the help they need.

Bulimics eat plenty of food, but they get rid of it by vomiting or using laxatives—they binge and purge. One girl lived with several friends in an apartment. Her friends noticed that this girl spent a long time in the bathroom every night after dinner. By chance, one of them walked by the bathroom door and heard her vomiting. When she came out, the friend asked if she was sick, but the girl laughed and denied she had been vomiting. The friend put two and two together and realized this girl was bulimic.

A third kind of eating disorder is very different from the other two. Some people are *compulsive overeaters.* They feel isolated and alone, so food becomes a friend that gives them a sense of warmth and satisfaction.

Anorexia, bulimia, and compulsive overeating are called "eating disorders," but they are really heart problems. They are ways people desperately try to gain control of their out-of-control life and fill the vacuum in their heart.

> . . . **go on crash diets.** Most doctors and nutritionists say that these diets do little if any good. The craving to lose weight in a hurry is another sign that a person is going too far. If you are significantly overweight, certainly you need to change your exercise and eating habits to promote better health. But if your weight is

relatively normal and you still feel the need to diet, that craving may signify a deeper need.

. . . **exercise compulsively.** It's great to be in shape, but some guys pump iron to make those bulging biceps just a little bit bigger than a friend's. And some girls run, Jazzercise, and do all kinds of workouts to have the flattest stomach in school. When people spend more time thinking about their appearance than developing relationships with others, that's unhealthy. And if being in shape is more important than having a relationship with Christ, that's sinful.

. . . **look like a slob.** Some people go the other direction. They eat and eat, and sit and sit. They don't do anything to take care of their body and look decent. Hey, you don't have to be a supermodel to look presentable! Some people, though, subconsciously want to be obese to keep people away from them. Because they fear intimacy, they reason that if they are fat enough, people won't want to get too close.

God gives each of us a certain body type. We can't change that. We can try like crazy, but it just won't work. A better solution is to thank God that he made you just the way you are. Accept yourself—then forget yourself. Stop comparing every curve and bulge to the Calvin Klein models!

David wrote about God's specific, hands-on purpose for creating each of us. He said: "You made all the delicate, inner parts of my body and knit me together in my mother's womb. Thank you for making me so wonderfully complex! Your workmanship is marvelous—and how well I know it. You watched me as I was being formed in utter seclusion, as I was woven together in the dark of the womb. You saw me before I was born. Every day of my life was recorded in your book. Every moment was laid out before a single day had passed" (Psalm 139:13-16).

God created your eyes, the shape of your nose, your height, your big feet, and everything else about you. His job was to create you in his infinite wisdom, grace, and love. And he did just that. Your job is to take care of his creation. Don't despise your body, and don't despise God for the way he made you. He has a plan for everything he does, so he created you the way he did for a reason. You can be sure his plan is good and right and loving.

If you can't stop obsessing about your shape, talk to your youth pastor or counselor about your problem. Eating disorders can be deadly—some young people have actually died as a result of them. At the very least, such disorders signify deep hurts that need to be healed. Besides that, thinking about yourself all the time (and being dissatisfied most of that time) isn't good for your emotional health or your relationships.

Remembering this might help:

Accept yourself—then forget yourself. Don't despise your body, and don't despise God for the way he made you.

50

How can I stop feeling so ashamed of myself?

SHAME MAY BE THE DEEPEST, and potentially the most destructive, human emotion. It may also be the most misunderstood and most unrecognized feeling that people experience. Shame wears many disguises, not always looking the way we expect it to look.

For instance, a person who lives the addicted lifestyle of a street alcoholic could certainly be said to be affected by shame, but so is the young person who is driven to dominate in everything he does, including relationships. Shame may be obvious in the background of a shy, isolated, and vulnerable young female who seems fearful of exposure. But shame may also be present, although less obvious, in her same-age friend who appears grandiose, self-centered, and confident. Losers who constantly feel guilty and condemned may have no more shame than popular people who are controlling, blaming, and manipulative.

The media have now made it difficult, if not impossible, to ignore the darker side of humanity. Everything seems to be "out of the closet," including addictions of every kind, physical and sexual abuse, and abortion. It's doubtful that the shame and guilt of such actions will ever again be entirely relegated to the secrecy of the closet.

What is shame, what is guilt, and how do they differ?

A primary difference is that shame has to do with a person's being while guilt has to do with a person's behavior. Shame involves the exposure of who we are, of that which is personal, private, or protected. For example, we don't want our bodies, our personal limitations, or our needs for worth, love, security, belonging, and dependency exposed inadvertently. This has to do with our identity.

When we feel exposed, we are vulnerable to criticism, ridicule, and condemnation. We fear others' judgment because we sense that if we are found lacking, we will be devalued or abandoned. This leads to a feeling of worthlessness. Shame also rears its ugly head when we simply remember an experience of exposure and devaluation.

While guilt focuses on our behavior and says, "I failed," shame deals with our being or our worth and says, "I am a failure." For those who feel ashamed and worthless, there seems to be no amount of penance that can cancel the debt. The person experiences an escalating cycle of shame, fear of abandonment, anger over the abandonment, guilt over the anger felt toward the person, then more shame, more guilt, and the downward spiral continues.

Shame can develop very early in a person's life. A child may receive messages such as, "You aren't good enough!" "You can't do anything right!" "You're a pain! I wish you'd go away!" Sometimes these messages are communicated verbally, but often they're communicated nonverbally through rolled eyes, a sarcastic remark and a shake of the head, or a simple turning away with a frown. If these are the predominant messages a child receives, it isn't long before she concludes, "I'm a really bad person. Nobody loves me, and nobody *should* love somebody as bad as I am." That conclusion is the essence of destructive, oppressive shame.

I have a friend who is very competent and very successful, but I've heard her say a million times, "I can't do anything right!" Her sense of shame robs her of the joy of living and the feeling of accomplishment. She is driven to do everything perfectly, and when she doesn't quite succeed, she condemns herself. One time I asked her, "When you blow it, what names do you call yourself?"

Her eyes widened as she looked at me. It was as if I had read her mind. She said, "You really don't want to know."

Severely condemning yourself every time you aren't perfect is a sure sign of shame.

Abandonment, of course, is a very clear, destructive message that a child isn't worth loving. Abandonment also sets a person up for expecting a lifetime of more abandonment, and this prophesy usually is proven true because the person chooses friends and lovers who only use them instead of loving them. For example, someone who was abandoned by her father may be attracted to someone who possesses the father's traits. This is an unconscious effort to "fix" the original relationship and get what was missing. Tragically, the person who possesses the undependable father's traits is not very likely to be dependable! And abandonment strikes again.

Abuse of any kind indicates to a child that he or she is an object of contempt, of no value except maybe to meet the abuser's needs. Strange as it may seem, though, abused kids often see their experience as normal, no matter how awful it is. They see their abusive parents as the source of love and value. That's how abuse totally skews children's perceptions of themselves, love, relationships, and God. No wonder they have a hard time relating to God!

When we think of abuse, we normally think of physical

abuse. Physical abuse comes in several forms and intensities, ranging from a spanking to satisfy the anger of a normally kind parent to atrocious cult-ritual abuse in which unimaginable horrors are committed. Many abuses are performed under the influence of an addictive substance.

Abuse may also be verbal or emotional. Verbal abuse includes yelling, name-calling, humiliation, comparison, and criticism aimed at the child rather than at his behavior. Emotional abuse includes lying to a child, ignoring him, discounting the child's emotions and needs, having excessive expectations, showing disgust toward the child, or blaming the child for things he or she is not responsible for. "Emotional incest" may also occur. Here is an example: A male child is promoted to adult responsibilities to meet his mother's adult needs for intimacy and companionship because the father is physically or emotionally unavailable.

The most damaging of all abuse is probably sexual abuse. Sexual abuse occurs whenever someone uses a child for his own stimulation. It runs the gamut from abuse of the privacy boundary in the home to inappropriate comments, exposure to pornography, and certainly to any kind of touching for the abuser's arousal. It says to a child, "You are useful to me as a sexual object but worthless as a person." Unfortunately, the primary bait used to lure most victims into the experience is an offer of emotional intimacy, which in shameful families is precisely what children crave the most.

What effects do all of these shaming experiences have on children? Shame builds and feeds on itself, and as one layer of shame stacks on the others, it becomes progressively more difficult to admit that the situation exists—much less to stop it. Abused children learn a model for perceiving and relating that is based on shame. This is true also for children whose parents express self-pity, helplessness, rage, or an intense drive to succeed.

How do shamed people survive? They find ingenious survival techniques to protect themselves so they can cope with unpleasant thoughts, memories, and feelings. All of us use these techniques from time to time, but it is very unhealthy to use them as a routine or rigid way of dealing with shame and anxiety. Examples include: denial (in which facts or events are excluded from reality); repression of feelings, perceptions, and memories (pushing them into the unconscious); and dissociation (a disengagement from reality in which the person imagines himself or herself as being somewhere else).

One of the most useful concepts for understanding how a person copes with shame is described by Robert McGee in his book *The Search for Significance.* He explains that people with low self-worth are easily deceived by Satan "into believing that the basis of their worth is their performance and their ability to please others."[1] Satan convinces people filled with shame that in order to be worthy, they must do something to earn worth.

A person who compulsively strives to perform better and gain approval might become the family hero, the school's star athlete, and later in life, the boss's favorite. Although this might seem pretty good, the person never gains permanent worth. Worthlessness always seems to be just one failure away. Shame is continually repeated due to the fear of failure or rejection—and certainly due to actual failure.

Addictions are also unhealthy ways of dealing with shame. What they offer the victim of shame is the myth of control. Being able to control feeling good, if even for a short while, seems well worth the consequences. Addiction comes in many forms, and it is not limited to *substances,* such as alcohol, drugs, or food. People can also be addicted to *experiences,* such as gambling, shopping, religion, sex, perfectionism, and relationships. People can even be addicted to *internal substances or activities,* such as adrenaline (thrill-seeking), fantasy, worry, and rage. All of these addictions offer the same myth: I can control myself, others, and events; therefore, I can meet my own needs.

How can we resolve shame? Here are some important elements:

Being honest.

Honesty is a key to unlock the door to recovery. The healing journey can begin only after people allow honest exposure of who they really are. Remember, though, that this is where shame begins, with exposure of the self. It is ironic that without this same exposure, no healing can come. A person must risk exposure to regain a connection with others. Revealing the true self should be done with a trustworthy and confidential person or group, such as a counselor or support group. It shouldn't be rushed. Most of us have layers upon layers of defenses, repressed memories, and feelings that cover up other memories and feelings. We should be patient with ourselves—just as God is. He will reveal to us what we need to expose, one thing at a time.

Some of us have grown up believing that repentance includes self-degradation or condemnation. Legitimate sorrow over the direction of our past actions doesn't require self-condemnation. Repenting shouldn't be a morbid, negative experience. Instead, it should be a positive time of using our free will to accept our God-given power to change.

Replacing the old with the new.

In Colossians 3:12-15 we are told that it is not enough to simply turn from our old ways. We must turn to or "clothe" ourselves with something new. We turn from our old thought patterns of self-hatred and self-pity, and we turn to the truth of God's grace, love, and strength.

Reestablishing intimacy.

We were created for intimacy with God, and we crave it when it's missing. Reestablishing that intimacy often happens only after we experience intimacy in a family setting and experience unconditional love. It is as if we must experience creature love before we can understand and accept the Creator's love. In some families that intimacy has been lost. Instead, we've learned dishonesty and secret keeping, and we've developed distrust. Our ability to express emotion has been disabled. In such cases, it is in a substitute family, a support group, that intimacy can be relearned, secrets revealed, trust restored, and emotions expressed.

Only God can orchestrate healing from shame. During the process, we must realize that others may hurt us again but we can always count on God to see us through.

Remembering this might help:

We should be patient with ourselves—just as God is.

NOTES
1. Robert McGee, *The Search for Significance* (Dallas, Tex.: Word, 1990).

51

I'm having a hard time trusting people. What can I do?

ONE OF THE MOST IMPORTANT LESSONS people need to learn is that trust must be earned. Sometimes we have a hard time trusting someone because that person has repeatedly betrayed us and isn't trustworthy. Trusting untrustworthy people isn't a virtue. It's foolish.

The problem comes when we have been betrayed and hurt deeply by someone, and the pain of our experience with that one person makes us reluctant to trust *anybody*. The problem then is more than the fact that some people around us aren't trustworthy. The bigger problem is that we aren't able to trust even those people who *are* trustworthy.

My friend Pat Springle wrote a book called *Trusting: Learning Who and How to Trust Again.*[1] In this book Pat describes four patterns of trust and mistrust. They are:

1. *Passive distrust.* People with this pattern have given up on trusting anybody. Their goal in any stressful relationship is to give in and get away. Instead of standing up for themselves, they just want to get the conflict over with as soon as possible, so they say, "Oh, do whatever you want. I don't care." Their other defense is to get away from anyone who may threaten them. They have thick walls to protect them from pain, but these walls

also prevent them from taking the risk to build good, loving relationships.

2. *Aggressive distrust.* These people have been betrayed and hurt deeply also, but their response is the opposite of the passive people. They defiantly refuse to ever be hurt again, so they are determined to be on top, to be in control, and to dominate every situation and every person. Often these are charming people—until they feel that someone has crossed them! Then the fangs come out, the eyes glare, and the venom drips from their mouths! (OK, so that's a bit exaggerated, but not much!)

3. *Blind trust.* Some people have a completely different response to betrayal: They don't want to face the fact that the person they trusted let them down, so they choose to trust that person anyway! Blind trusters desperately want to please, so they close their eyes to addictive, abusive behavior around them, and they trust the untrustworthy.

4. *Perceptive trust.* And some people are wise and discerning. They have their eyes open and can see (or at least learn to see) who is trustworthy and who is not. This is the essence of what the Bible calls wisdom. The goals of wise people are to be honest and loving and to make the hard choices of when and how to take calculated risks in relationships.

If you are having trouble trusting people, the problem may be that the people around you aren't trustworthy. Or the problem may be that your "truster" is broken and you can't trust even those who deserve your trust. Maybe both problems exist, each in different situations. Ultimately, God is the only one who is always trustworthy. Even when we don't understand his ways, we can be sure of his good and gracious intentions.

Find someone to talk to about your deep hurts. Trust can be shattered, but it can also be rebuilt and restored. It takes time and attention, but it's worth it.

Remembering this might help:

Make it a goal to be wise and discerning about who is trustworthy and who is not.

NOTES

1. Pat Springle, *Trusting: Learning Who and How to Trust Again* (Ann Arbor, Mich.: Servant, 1994).

52

I just want to avoid people. Being around them hurts too much. Who can I turn to?

WHEN I DO CONCERTS, I give people everything I've got. I sing up a storm, and when it's over, I come out to say, "Hey!" to people and sign autographs. After that, though, I've had it. I'm exhausted, and I don't want to see anybody about anything at all. It's not that I don't care about people or that I don't like them. I love them! But at that point, I'm "peopled out." I'm sweaty and tired. I can't take another hug, another handshake, or another smile. I've had it! I need to get away.

Have you ever had someone bump into you in the hall at school? Of course you have. If your arm was just barely touched, it didn't hurt at all. If you were hit a little harder, it might cause a little discomfort, but the pain would go away very quickly. Why? Because your arm was healthy and well. But what if your arm were broken? Ouch! You would have a doctor put a cast on it immediately to protect your arm from further injury. You wouldn't wait until someone bumped into it to get it fixed. With an unhealthy arm, even the slightest touch would be agony, so you'd pull back from people or things that might cause you more pain.

If it is hard for you to be around people, it is because your spirit has been broken and wounded like that injured arm. The walls you have built around you are like the cast. You think they will protect you from getting hurt again. Unlike an arm in a cast, though, your spirit can't heal behind walls.

The story begins like this: You get hurt by someone. The only way the wound in your spirit can heal is to forgive that person. But you don't forgive, so the open wound just gets worse. Now you're walking around with an infected scar, and someone else offends you. The sore gets larger and more painful. It doesn't take a hard hit to bring you pain. Even the slightest offense is agony because your spirit is wounded and sick.

Eventually you get tired of the constant pain, so you put a cast on your spirit. You build a protective wall around yourself and withdraw from anyone who might hurt you.

Some of us have been hurt so deeply that we withdraw from any kind of interaction with others. We are simply too afraid of being hurt again. The risk is too great. Others of us spend our life giving, helping, and serving others. From the outside, we may appear to be the most social people in the world, but inside we are lonely. Our attempts to please others by helping and serving are designed to win affection. Though we may occasionally see a glimpse of love and respect, it quickly fades. Then, thinking we have been abandoned by both people and God, we feel empty and companionless. We distrust authority, believing that anyone above us is against us, and we build elaborate facades to hide our painful feelings of loneliness.

Sarah described her relationship with her cold, rigid, demanding boyfriend. She longed for his acceptance and affection, but what she got was a physical relationship and shallow conversation. In return, he expected her to drop whatever she was doing to do whatever he wanted. Sarah's conclusion was that the problem was her fault. "I guess I'm just not a good person," she said weakly, looking down. "I guess I'm not worthy of being loved." She began to cry.

Abusive or addicted people usually give a little and take a lot. In contrast, many of us are like a tank of water with a slow drip coming in and a stream going out. For a while, the tank will flow, but eventually it runs dry. The trickle can never fill the tank as long as there is a big hole in the bottom. We may get a little encouragement, but we give so much more time and emotional energy that we are effectually "running on empty."

As we give and give, a destructive sense of entitlement, "you owe me," grows within us. We feel entitled to the appreciation and respect of others. Getting strokes becomes a compulsion. When we get that appreciation and respect, we are satisfied like an alcoholic taking a drink. When we don't get it, we feel angry and abandoned. We feel condemned. We feel controlled. We feel confused. We feel lonely. We feel angry, but we can't say anything or we might experience even more condemnation, manipulation, and loneliness. We feel hopelessly trapped.

Afraid of our emotions, we stuff them and act as if nothing is wrong. We are unwilling to say how we feel—that we are hurt and angry—because we are afraid that people will withdraw from us. We're afraid they will go away, and we'll be even more lonely. Worse than that, if we don't act as if we appreciate what they say and do, they will probably get angry with us, and that risk is simply too great. We are lonely now, and we don't want to feel any more lonely.

"OK," you say, "so I need someone who will affirm and encourage me, be honest with me, and model a real and healthy life. But who?" Good question! You may already know someone who can help you, or it may take some looking. You may not know anybody right now who can be that kind of friend. For some of us, our "friends" are a major part of the problems we are experiencing. But for others, friends can provide the understanding and patience we need to help us heal and grow.

Your youth pastor can probably help you find a friend, or he may direct you to a group. Or you may want to find a qualified Christian counselor to help you. The person you select will be determined by a number of factors, including his or her availability and schedule, and your desire. You may want the professional care and confidentiality of a counselor, but be sure that you find one whose counseling is based on biblical principles.

There is a stigma about counseling in the minds of some people. They believe that "all counselors are quacks" and that you have to be "really messed up" to go to one. Not everybody needs to go to a counselor, but many people would benefit from the warmth, affirmation, and objectivity that a good counselor can provide.

The grip of loneliness is strong—you were not meant to make it on your own. So pray that God will show you how to find friends who will "be there" for you . . . and whom you can help to support. You'll both be glad you found one another!

Remembering this might help:

You might be one of the many people who would benefit from the warmth, affirmation, and objectivity that a good counselor can provide.

53

Somebody close to me died. Sometimes I feel numb. Sometimes I feel rage. What's going on?

IF I HAD KNOWN WE WERE GOING to go down in that plane, I would have said a lot of things to my friend who died in the crash. I would have told him how much I cared about him, how much I appreciated him. I would have told him and showed him a lot more love and appreciation than I did. I am asked questions every day about what happened, and every day I wish I'd told him more. I wrote the song that says,

> You'll never know how much I lost losing you.
> If you only knew.
> There's not a day that goes by
> That I don't think of you and ask God why
> I won't get the chance to tell you, "Good-bye,"
> Or how much I lost losing you.
> If you only knew.

People need to grieve when a relative or close friend dies, for there is justifiable sadness. We feel a deep sense of loss, a deep emptiness. There are so many things we wish we'd said, so many things we wish we'd done. And now we can't.

These wounds hurt deeply, and sadness often leads to anger. We're angry because we couldn't control what happened and we can't bring the person back.

If the sense of loss is left ungrieved, the hurt and anger fester and foul virtually every aspect of our life. We may explode in rage. We may implode in depression by turning our anger inward. We may resort to alcohol, food, drugs, sex, gambling, perfectionism, "fixing" people, or a host of other avenues that deaden the pain and give us some sense of security. All of these things, however, prevent us from finding real solutions. They keep us from facing the original pain and grieving our deep losses. The losses we feel because someone died are then combined with losses that are self-inflicted.

Effectively dealing with traumatic, emotional difficulties includes five stages: denial, bargaining, anger, grief, and acceptance. This is not a push-button, one-two-three kind of process. People may move quickly through one phase but very slowly through another. And they may go back and forth from time to time, reentering a stage they have already gone through as they become aware of other pains and hurts they have not previously seen. Generally speaking, however, people will not progress to the next stage until they have more or less fully experienced the one they're in.

If we lose someone to a terminal illness, we may have gone through a denial period while the person was alive. During this time we may have tried to reassure ourselves: "He isn't really that sick." "God won't let him die." "He'll be better soon. You'll see."

Bargaining usually occurs also before a person dies from a long, terminal illness. It is an expression of hope—hope that the other person will somehow get better, hope that the cancer will go away if we pray the right way. But it is usually a false hope. The hard truth, the reality of objective observation, leads us to a painful but honest conclusion: We need to give up. Giving up doesn't sound very spiritual, but it is. Giving up is a reflection of reality about a terminal illness. Certainly it is good to pray and ask God for a miracle. Sometimes God grants healing; but often God's miracle is that we feel his presence, comfort, and love in the midst of our loss.

To understand how we get from bargaining to acceptance, you may find it helpful to picture the following diagram in your mind. Objectivity is the door that opens into the process. Acceptance is the door leading out of it and into health. In the middle are three containers, which represent bargaining, anger, and grief. People usually will not progress to constructive anger until they're through with bargaining, and they probably won't experience grief until they have spent their anger.

After the person dies, we may go through denial again. Obviously, there is nothing for which to bargain anymore, so the denial is now followed immediately by anger, grief, and acceptance.

- *Denial.* Some us us become passive and emotionally numb in our effort to block the pain of losing someone. We avoid decisions and relationships. Some of us are so crushed, so hopeless, so depressed, that we don't believe anything good can or will ever happen to us. We withdraw into a cocoon of morbid introspection and discouragement.

- *Anger.* We get angry at ourselves for not doing enough. We get angry at the doctors for failing to save the person's life. We get angry at the dead person for abandoning us. We get angry at God for letting the person die. And we get angry at ourselves for being angry.

- *Grief.* When our anger is spent, a sense of loss begins to dominate us. We grieve. We had something precious, and it was taken away. Or we realize that we had wanted something—love and acceptance from a certain person—very badly but will never have it. We wanted intimacy, warmth, and laughter, but we feel only hurt and emptiness.
- *Acceptance.* Finally, we experience a sense of peace and calm. The bargaining, anger, and grief have been exposed and expressed. We are objective about life: its goodness and badness, its righteousness and wickedness. We are uncomfortable with simple, easy answers, knowing that they just don't work. We gain a new depth in our relationship with the Lord and with people. We discover new perspectives on life, new values, and new lifestyles.

We live in an instant society. We don't like to wait. We want to be comfortable. So we conclude that pain and grief, especially over a long period of time, are bad. We've been trained to expect that we can have what we want quickly and painlessly. It's no wonder that grieving a death is considered a nuisance. Some well-meaning people tell us, "It's been three months since your father died. Get over it!" People who help others in the grieving process tell us that it takes about two years to grieve a major loss such as the death of someone we love. Be realistic. Take your time. Be honest with yourself and with someone who can help you through the process. We need to let the Lord communicate his love and grace to us. We need to let him be "our refuge and strength, always ready to help in times of trouble" (Psalm 46:1).

Remembering this might help:

Effectively dealing with traumatic, emotional difficulties includes denial, bargaining, anger, grief, and acceptance.

54

Why am I so angry all the time? Is anger sin?

SEVERAL YEARS AGO A CLOSE FRIEND of mine lied to me. I had trusted him. We had been as close as brothers. Maybe closer. But one day out of nowhere I found out he had been two-faced. That was bad, but what happened next was worse. I really believe we could have worked through the lie; but instead of admitting he lied, he blamed me! I'd like to tell you I got over this very quickly and easily, but that would be a lie too. It was hard. I was furious at this guy for a long, long time.

You might be bitter

- . . . at one of your parents for showing preference toward your brother or sister.
- . . . at both of your parents for splitting up and ruining your family.
- . . . at a teacher for being so unfair.
- . . . at a trusted friend for telling other people a secret you had confided.
- . . . at a boyfriend or girlfriend for dumping you or using you.
- . . . at yourself for some dumb choice you made.
- . . . at God because you think he let you down when you needed him.

Unresolved anger reaches into every aspect of our life, for our minds can't stop reliving the wound. We may secretly plan our revenge or deny that the wound ever happened. Our emotions become trapped in the vise grip of fear, hurt, and anger. Then we can't respond to life spontaneously and have fun. Our range of emotions shrinks to a narrow rut. Our relationships are shaped and colored by seeing people as for us or against us. We demand their loyalty, and we viciously denounce them or withdraw from them if they disappoint us. We become angry at God (though we may not admit it) because we believe he let us down.

Our body is affected by our bitterness. Our sleep or eating habits may be disrupted. We have tight muscles and bad headaches. The acid in our stomach churns and burns as our rage attacks us from the inside. If our anger becomes too intense for our body's tolerance of stress, our body may shut down. At that point we will experience the ten-ton weight of lethargy and depression.

These consequences of bitterness are very real and very serious. We need to understand the importance of dealing appropriately with the powerful but misunderstood emotion of anger.

Not all anger is wrong, nor is all anger right. Some of it is good and wholesome, but much of it is sin. There is a difference between feeling angry and acting in an angry manner. It isn't wrong to feel angry when it is a natural response to injustice. Some people see this anger as sin, and they either deny that it exists or they express it indirectly (passive aggression) and inappropriately. Our expression of anger can be either righteous or unrighteous. It can either hurt or heal. Two classic passages about anger are found in Ephesians 4 and James 1.

Paul acknowledges that we will feel anger but tells us not to express that anger unrighteously: "'Don't sin by letting anger gain control over you.' Don't let the sun go down while you are still angry, for anger gives a mighty foothold to the Devil" (Ephesians 4:26-27).

James warns us not to let our expression of anger hurt others: "My dear brothers and sisters, be quick to listen, slow to speak, and slow to get angry. Your anger can never make things right in God's sight" (James 1:19-20).

There's a difference between *constructive* anger and *destructive* anger. Constructive anger is the feeling of anger at injustice. This kind of anger leads to positive, constructive steps, such as speaking the truth to the person who hurt us and forgiving that person. Destructive anger is based on the desire to harm another person. It consists of outbursts, rage, seething, and revenge. Too often we cross over the line in our response, and the feeling of anger quickly becomes destructive. That's why Paul said not to let your anger (constructive anger) gain control over you (destructive anger).

In Paul's message to the Ephesians, there are three things you need to know:

1. Anger is a God-given emotion.
2. Anger is not necessarily sinful.
3. Anger must have safeguards.

These are the safeguards found in Ephesians 4:

- *"Don't let the sun go down while you are still angry."* In other words, do not prolong anger into the night. Make sure you solve your anger problem by the end of the day.

- *Don't let your anger give a "foothold to the Devil."* That means: Don't express your anger in such a way that the devil gets his foot in the door of your life. This happens when we refuse to be honest about our hurt or when we refuse to forgive. Then our anger turns to bitterness and we want revenge, not forgiveness.

Dr. Archibald Hart, dean of the Graduate School of Psychology at Fuller Seminary, identifies four distinct causes of anger:

1. Frustration—caused by blocked goals
2. Hurt—physical or psychological offenses
3. Conditional responses—anger that is programmed into us
4. Instinctive protection—our responses to dangerous life situations[1]

Anger that is not dealt with in the right way can destroy you. You can be free of constant anger if you find the real reason for the anger, face it honestly, then work through the problem. You should go directly to any person who is causing you frustration and respectfully tell him or her what is making you angry.

Unfortunately, these are some typical ways we respond to intense feelings of anger:

- *Numbness.* "I don't want to feel this way, so I won't." This is a personal philosophy for some of us. Our pain is too great, so we block it out. Our anger is too frightening, so we act as if it's not there. We are forced to live life at the surface emotionally because what's underneath is simply too much to bear. We have superficial emotions and superficial relationships.

- *Pain without gain.* Some of us may wish we were numb, but we aren't. We hurt. We hurt so badly we can hardly stand it. There is a feeling of being crushed—hopelessly crushed. An intense feeling of loss with no hope of gain consumes us. We feel as though we've been broken into a million pieces, and there isn't any glue to fix us. No healing; only hurt. Because we can't go through life admitting this kind of hurt to others, we put up a facade of competence and happiness. Few people ever realize the blackness that lurks beneath our neon outside.

- *Excuses for the offender and blame for ourselves.* Some of us blame anybody and everybody except the person who actually hurt us. The offender is excused for his or her offense. The desire to "believe the best" of the one who has hurt us blocks our objectivity. Instead of blaming the other person, we blame ourselves.

- *Outbursts of anger.* In addition to getting angry at the wrong thing or person, we may also become disproportionately angry. Our suppressed anger may explode like a tube of toothpaste that is squeezed until it pops and toothpaste squirts in all directions.

I know a guy who is an explosion waiting to happen! He goes along fairly well for a while until something knocks him over the edge. Then watch out! He tries to hide his outbursts of rage, but I see broken things in his apartment from time to time. He doesn't want to talk about it because he is so ashamed of being out of control. But if he doesn't talk about it, he won't get the help he needs. What is he angry about? I certainly don't know, and I'm not sure he knows. I suspect it is something really painful that happened a long time ago that he has never resolved.

- *Self-pity and anger that manipulates others.* Hurt and anger are powerful emotions. They affect us deeply and can be used to affect others, too. They can be powerful forces of manipulation to get others to care about us and dance to our tune.

If you're angry most of the time, the reason is probably more serious than any of the ones listed above. You need a pastor, school counselor, or a Christian counselor who can help you find the root of your problem.

Repressing our hurt and anger, excusing those who hurt us, scapegoating others, and mindlessly venting our rage are unproductive ways to try to cope with our anger. If our anger is triggered by our unrealistic expectations, then we need more realistic ones. We also need to develop a tolerance for disappointment. If, however, our anger is a response to past or present hurts, we need to learn to forgive. (For a detailed look at forgiveness, see the next question, number 55.)

Anger is like a pair of dark sunglasses. It changes the way everything looks and keeps you from seeing things the way they really are. Anger hardens your heart toward God until you can no longer hear him. It hardens your heart toward other people and keeps you from seeing their pain. Once you remove these sunglasses of anger, you'll begin to see life and people in a completely different way.

The evidence of the Holy Spirit in your life is love, joy, peace, and self-control. Unchecked anger will rob you of those things. Don't let that happen. Don't waste your life being angry. *Anger is not worth the price you pay to hold on to it.* You can choose to let go of your anger and let God begin to heal you. Ask him to lead you now to someone who can help you.

Remembering this might help:

"Don't sin by letting anger gain control over you" (Ephesians 4:26).

NOTES

1. Dr. Archibald Hart, *Rapha Newsletter* (Houston, Tex.: Rapha, January 1993).

55

How can I forgive someone who has hurt me really badly?

WHEN MY GOOD FRIEND BETRAYED me years ago, it hurt really badly. For a while, I sulked and got depressed. Then all the passages in the Bible about forgiveness started coming back to me. I knew I had to forgive. That's when I wrote the song "To Forgive." I still have a ways to go in forgiving this friend, but God has allowed me to take a lot of steps in the right direction.

Many Christians find it difficult to forgive. Here are two important things to know about forgiveness:

1. *Forgiveness is not something you do when you feel like it.* True, biblical forgiveness is an act of your will. It is something you choose to do no matter how you feel. It is an act of obedience to God.

2. *Forgiveness is undeserved pardon.* Don't wait until a person asks for your forgiveness. That will be too late. Jesus offered us forgiveness when we didn't deserve it. Real forgiveness is not deserved or earned. Maybe you're saying to yourself, *But that's not fair! I get all the pain and the person that hurt me goes free.* I hear you. But Jesus took all your pain on the cross, and you went free. He is our example. That's real forgiveness. When you release someone from the debt that person owes you,

you free yourself of the responsibility to convict the person of guilt. That's the Holy Spirit's job.

Compassionate people are always ready to forgive because they realize that they, too, will someday need the forgiveness of another person. Forgiveness is not excusing or forgetting what happened. It is not a feeling. It is a choice we make to give up the right to get even and to release feelings of anger or hurt.

If you choose not to forgive, understand that you will pay a big price. Not forgiving will corrode your disposition, elevate your blood pressure, upset your digestive system, ulcerate your stomach, and perhaps bring on a nervous breakdown or a heart attack. Bitterness is serious business.

An unforgiving spirit can also cause you not to be able to trust or love unconditionally. It will make it more difficult to pray. Over time, not forgiving those who hurt you can lead to depression, anger, rage, and violence, as well as mental and emotional illness.

Bitterness is anger that has been repressed and has festered. Over weeks, months, and years, anger from unforgiven wounds and injustices simmers in its own venom, increasing until it consumes the angry person.

Bitterness is expressed in several ways:

- Hating others
- Hating ourselves
- Displaying rage
- Hating God

Love transforms. So does bitterness. Love stimulates creativity and freshness of thought; it energizes people to care for others and brings affirmation and freedom. Love builds. In contrast, bitterness destroys. It sucks the freshness out of life and focuses attention and efforts on getting even and hurting others.

Anger's initial motive may be justice. But rather than seeking a just solution that is ultimately constructive, hatred seeks to wound, hurt, humiliate, and destroy. And it is very successful when expressed through verbal and nonverbal condemnation, sarcasm and outright ridicule, attacks and abandonment.

Jealousy of others' successes is only a half step away from hatred. When people compare themselves to others and thus perceive themselves as deficient, the resulting anger can easily turn into hatred—and a desire to hurt the one who has shown them up.

But in their passion to hurt others, those who lash out in bitterness hurt themselves, too. At the very least, they waste precious time on negative, harmful exercises. Usually, though, the tragedy of hatred is much more costly. It consumes people with a passion for revenge that may eventually cause depression or various psychosomatic illnesses.

Admitting hatred is a big step, but it is only one step toward genuine, emotional health. Though they need to keep growing, some people get stuck after this admission.

People often fail to forgive others (and themselves) because they don't think it's possible. They forget that God has graciously forgiven all his children's sins through Christ's death, and they rationalize why they can't forgive. In *The Search for Significance,* Robert McGee lists several ways people rationalize their unwillingness to forgive themselves and others:

1. The offense was too great.
2. They don't agree that they have offended me.

3. They aren't truly sorry.
4. They never asked to be forgiven.
5. They'll do it again.
6. They did it again.
7. I don't like them.
8. They did it deliberately.
9. If I forgive them, I'll have to treat them right.
10. Someone has to punish them.
11. Something keeps me from forgiving.
12. I'll be a hypocrite if I forgive, because I don't feel like it.
13. I'll forgive, but I won't forget.
14. I have forgiven a lesser offense, after excusing the real offense.[1]

Being offended or hurt by others is a frequent experience in life. The hurt comes from experiencing an offense and then reliving it. In fact, the initial pain usually amounts to only a small fraction of the total hurt. The majority of the pain comes afterward as people dwell on the offense and their reaction to it. This can be avoided when they learn to deal with offenses rather than relive them countless times.

When someone hurts another person, a debt is incurred. A sense of justice cries out, "He owes me!" Love and justice are the cornerstones of emotional stability.

Forgiveness, which is releasing someone from a debt, doesn't come naturally. It seems awkward, at best; to some it seems absurd.

The Christian has a unique capacity for forgiveness because he can appropriate the forgiveness of the Cross. God has forgiven us fully and completely. We, of all people, should be aware of what it is like to experience unconditional forgiveness. As a result, we should in turn be able to forgive those around us. Think of it this way: There is nothing that anyone can do to me (insult me, lie about me, annoy me, etc.) that can compare with what Christ has forgiven me for doing. We gain a better perspective of others' offenses when we compare them to our sin of rebellion that Christ has completely forgiven. In Ephesians 4:32 Paul writes, "Be kind to each other, tenderhearted, forgiving one another, just as God through Christ has forgiven you."

When I have a hard time forgiving somebody, I try to remember the cross. If Jesus was willing to go to the cross and die that horrible death to forgive my sins, I can be willing to forgive those who hurt me. That doesn't mean I feel no hurt when people lie to me or offend me, but remembering the cross gives me perspective and motivation to say, "Yeah, you did this to me, but I've done a lot worse, and Jesus has forgiven me for it. So I forgive you."

The ability to forgive is tied to that kind of personal experience of Christ's forgiveness (Colossians 3:13). To put it another way, we will be unable to truly forgive others for their sins toward us if we don't experience forgiveness for our own sins toward God and others.

This realization is a turning point. Many people have repressed their hurt for years. They've been afraid of the rage they have glimpsed in themselves from time to time, and they have sensed an overwhelming emptiness and hopelessness lurking in the recesses of their heart. They have been wounded. They have been wronged. They are victims.

This "victim mentality" can become so pervasive that the victims don't assume responsibility for their own sinful behavior. They are victims, but they are also victimizers.

How do you forgive someone who has hurt you badly? First tell the person eye to eye what he or she did that hurt you. Don't worry about the response. Then say to yourself (and perhaps to the other person), "I choose to forgive you, [name], for _____, and I release you to Jesus." That simple act of obedience begins the process of healing in your life. It's not a magic wand, and it may not happen overnight, but the healing will come eventually.

You hear some people say, "Forgive and forget." Well, forgiveness does not make you lose your memory, but forgiveness takes the sting out of the memory of what the person did. You still remember what happened, but it doesn't hurt as much anymore.

Forgiveness provides a platform to develop a relationship if both parties are willing. If the other person insists on having a relationship with you only on his or her terms, you should refuse to be manipulated or controlled again. However, through your forgiveness, you are offering the option to build a relationship established on respect and honesty.

Remembering this might help:

First tell the person eye to eye what he or she did that hurt you. Then say, "I choose to forgive you, [name], and I release you to Jesus."

NOTES
1. Robert McGee, *The Search for Significance* (book and workbook) (Dallas, Tex.: Word, 1990), 246.

56

How can I know God is really there for me?

AFTER THE PLANE CRASH, I was really angry at God for
a long time. This may sound strange, but anger at someone
implies that you have a relationship . . . you have expectations
. . . you have a significant connection with the person you're
mad at. My struggle with God during that time (blaming him,
feeling guilty for what happened, being confused about his
intentions) verified the fact that my relationship with God
was very strong.

I told my dad, "When I see Jesus for the first time, I'm going
to say: 'I want some answers about the crash, and I want them
now!'"

But Dad told me, "No, Son, when you see Jesus, you won't
say anything. You're going to bow to him, and I bet you'll
keep your mouth shut."

Dad was probably right, but he didn't have stitches and
scars in his face like I did. I was bitter. No, it's not pretty, but
it's the truth—I was bitter at God for allowing that plane crash.
Even so, God could handle my honesty. And because I could
be honest with God, our relationship grew even stronger. It
sounds odd, but I'm genuinely thankful for that time of bitterness because it deepened my relationship with God.

If you have trusted Christ as your Savior and you have a
relationship with Jesus, then God is your Father. You are his

kid. The same Bible that promises you eternal life also promises that God will never leave you (Hebrews 13:5) and that no one can take you away from him. Jesus said, "My sheep recognize my voice; I know them, and they follow me. I give them eternal life, and they will never perish. No one will snatch them away from me, for my Father has given them to me, and he is more powerful than anyone else. So no one can take them from me" (John 10:27-29). Sheep are dumb. That's why they need a shepherd. There are a lot of days when I'm just plain dumb. That's why I need a Shepherd too!

Sometimes you may not *feel* that God is there for you, but the facts say he is. The theological term for this is *divine immanence.* It means that God is personally present everywhere. When I doubt God's goodness and presence in my life, I have to ask myself: "Do I believe my feelings or do I believe God's Word?" Our feelings can change, but God and his Word are constant and true.

The Bible says God loves us, but why do many of us feel so distant from him? The unconditional love, forgiveness, and acceptance of God are the message we need; but instead, we sometimes feel as if he has deserted us. We feel that he doesn't approve of us and that we can't do enough to please him no matter how hard we try. This compounds our feelings of hopelessness, pain, and loneliness because God is our last hope: "If he doesn't love me, who will?"

Our view of God is almost always the same as our view of our parents. If our parents have neglected us, we will probably feel that God doesn't care. If our parents have condemned us, we will feel that God is harsh and demanding. In whatever way our parents have treated us, that is the perception we have of God, who then is seen as part of the problem, not the solution.

If you are having doubts about God's faithfulness, focus on getting to know him better. When you do, your faith and understanding of his ways will grow. No matter what your feelings are telling you, the fact of God's love and care remains true and unchangeable. Peter quoted an Old Testament verse in one of his letters: "The word of the Lord will last forever" (1 Peter 1:25).

Begin "practicing the presence" of the Lord in your life by asking God to make you sensitive to his presence. Make sure there aren't any barriers (any unconfessed sins) between you and your heavenly Father. Try to read from the Bible every day to get wisdom and encouragement. If you don't know where to start, begin with Leviticus. (Just kidding!) Start reading in John; then read some of Paul's letters, such as Ephesians, Colossians, and Galatians. Check out the Psalms, too. The psalmists wrote of their true feelings about life and God. Sometimes they were really thankful, and sometimes they were upset about being in the pits! (Sounds like my life!) Mark in your Bible every verse that has to do with God's presence or faithfulness, and thank him each day for those promises!

One of my favorite Bible passages is in Psalm 73. The writer, Asaph, has told God that he is ticked off at him. In fact, he's so mad that he can't see straight! Then he spends some time with God and gets a new perspective. He reflects on his experience of being so angry and feeling so distant from God:

> Then I realized how bitter I had become. . . . I was
> so foolish and ignorant—I must have seemed like
> a senseless animal to you. (Psalm 73:21-22)

Wow! He was so angry, he was like a wild animal! He felt distant from God, but God was right there, tenderly holding on to him:

Yet I still belong to you; you are holding my right hand. You will keep on guiding me with your counsel, leading me to a glorious destiny. (Psalm 73:23-24)

The writer then realizes how wonderful God's goodness to him is:

Whom have I in heaven but you? I desire you more than anything on earth. . . . How good it is to be near God! I have made the Sovereign Lord my shelter, and I will tell everyone about the wonderful things you do. (Psalm 73:25, 28)

When you and I feel like wild animals, God is still there for us, too. In fact, he's holding our hands. I like that!

Not long ago, a student walked into a school in Paducah, Kentucky, and shot several others who were praying. Dawson McAllister and I were asked to speak and sing at the memorial service. People asked, "Where was God when that boy opened fire? Doesn't he care?"

Dawson told them, "God was in the same place he was when people were crucifying his Son."

God cares, and he is sovereign, but not everything is clear to us now. There have been many situations in which I have wondered what God was doing—the plane crash, some friendships gone sour, other times when I've been hurt emotionally and physically. I'm convinced that one of the reasons (maybe the number one reason) we go through hard times is so we will turn to God and learn to depend on him. When life is too easy, we tend to forget about God. Problems show us how much we need him.

No matter what is going on in your life, I assure you: God is there. He's not asleep. And he's not confused. There has never been a time when something happened to you or me or anybody else and God said, "Well, hey, I didn't think *that* would happen!" No, he knows and he cares.

There are a lot of things about life that I don't understand yet, but there's one thing I'm absolutely sure of. Jesus is alive, and he loves you very, very much. You can count on that!

Remembering this might help:

The same Bible that promises you eternal life also promises that God will never leave you and that no one can take you away from him.

CoNClusioN

For Teenagers: Have Your Questions Been Answered?

I hope you've enjoyed reading this book, and I hope I've been able to answer your questions. Obviously, there are a zillion variations to each question, and I haven't tried to answer all of those. The main thing to remember is that if we keep asking, seeking, and knocking, God will open the door and give us what we need.

The Bible doesn't contain the answer to *every* question. (I always wished the answers to geometry tests were in there, but I never found them!) But the Scriptures contain all the principles we need to live a full, happy life that pleases God. Part of the adventure of the Christian life is that we have to dig to find the gold. We have to read the Bible, study what it says, and talk to other people so we can learn how to apply these truths to our specific situations. Don't know how? Look back at the question about how to study the Bible. That'll be a good start. And put yourself around people who really love God and know the Scriptures. Ask 'em questions till they turn blue! It'll be good for both of you.

Carve out time to pray and sing and develop your relationship with Jesus. Would you want to spend time with the most loving and powerful movie star or president or king? You bet! Well, Jesus is far greater and more loving than any of them! And he delights in you! Talk to him as your dearest friend . . . because that's exactly what he is.

Get involved with a good group of young people who genuinely follow Christ. Go on retreats and to conferences (and concerts, of course!) to encourage your faith. The more you dive into the deep waters of Christian friendships and Bible teaching, the richer your life will be.

Do you have some friends who need a few questions answered? Give them this book, and show them the specific question and answer that will be meaningful to them. Keep the book as a reference for yourself and your friends as you face challenges together. It would make me really happy to know that God is using my book like that!

Recommended Reading

Anderson, Neil T., and Dave Park. *The Bondage Breaker: Youth.* Eugene, Ore.: Harvest House, 1995.

Becker, Vern. *The Campus Life Guide to Dating.* Grand Rapids, Mich.: Zondervan, 1990.

Christian, S. Rickly. *Alive 1: Daily Devotions* and *Alive 2: Daily Devotions.* Grand Rapids, Mich.: Zondervan, 1995.

Hartman, Bob. *More Power to Ya: The Petra Devotional.* Cincinnati, Ohio: Standard, 1997.

McDowell, Josh, and Bill Jones. *The Teenage Question and Answer Book.* Dallas, Tex.: Word, 1990.

Peterson, Eugene H. *The Message: The New Testament in Contemporary English.* Colorado Springs, Colo.: NavPress, 1994.

Shealey, Dal, and Pat Springle. *One Way 2 Play.* Nashville, Tenn.: Thomas Nelson, 1995.

St. James, Rebecca. *You're the Voice.* Nashville, Tenn.: Thomas
Nelson, 1997.

The Student Bible, New International Version. Grand Rapids,
Mich.: Zondervan, 1992.

The Student Life Application Bible, New Living Translation.
Wheaton, Ill.: Tyndale House, 1996.

For Parents, Teachers, Friends, and Youth Leaders

Understanding Adolescence

Adolescence is a "rite of passage" from childhood into adult
life; but for most, that passage is a stormy one! Tremendous
changes are taking place. Hormones produce physical changes,
creating passions as well. Kids who only yesterday (it seems)
thought the opposite sex was "gross" now can't stop day-
dreaming about dates and . . . Young people experience dramatic changes in their relationships. Peers increasingly define
each other's sense of identity. Relationships with parents are
still vitally important, but you might not guess that from the
typical teenager's tone of voice and body language! This age
also produces changes in moral and spiritual values as the
young person wrestles with forming his or her own set of
beliefs, not just those inherited from parents. The struggles
and questions and experimentation are a normal, healthy part
of growing up—unless it all gets too extreme.

Of course, some young people glide through this maze
effortlessly and develop a strong identity, wisdom, direction,
and relationships in the process. Most, however, experience
a more difficult path. Some look to "heroes" to show them how
to act and what to value, and some try to define themselves
through name brands on clothes and cars. The ones who rebel

get the most press—and the most stares. They may turn to violence, or they may color their hair purple and pierce various body parts just to be different. All of them experiment with adult behaviors—after all, that's what they're trying to become. They need all the practice they can get! But all of them also need to feel that they belong somewhere. And all of them have questions that need to be answered. The question is: Who will they turn to for answers?

Becoming Safe . . .

It's relatively easy to be a person with answers. The much harder task is to be someone who is safe enough so young people will ask you their questions.

Here are some characteristics of people who are safe:

They display warmth. Young people study their peers and adults to read every raised eyebrow and every inflection in tone of voice. They want to see if they are accepted. If they aren't, these young people lock themselves up like a cabinet with a missing key. But if they feel loved and accepted, they will feel safe enough to open up. Unconditional acceptance and the determination to avoid condemnation are the foundation of building a trust relationship.

They show empathy. This is not just an accurate understanding of another person's predicament. Empathy involves feeling what other people feel. It is "walking in their shoes," so we genuinely identify with their struggles. Empathy builds trust because it allows young people to be who they are.

People who are safe are good listeners. A friend of mine told me, "It's not as important that a person *understand* as it is that the other person *feel understood.*" The way for people to feel understood is for us to listen to them. Sometimes we think we've figured out the problem, so we jump in to fix it as soon as possible. We would be much wiser to be patient, to look for the feelings behind the questions, and then to look for hidden questions under the more obvious ones. Adolescents often ask surface questions to see how they are handled. If they feel safe enough after that, they may take the risk of bringing up the issues that are really troubling them.

One of the ways a teenager can tell if we are really listening to them is if we ask "the second and third questions" to get more information. Another way to listen well is to reflect what people are saying back to them: "Here's what I hear you saying. . . ." We can also reflect feelings back to them, such as: "That hurt when you didn't make the team." When we patiently reflect people's statements and feelings back to them, they usually feel safe enough to volunteer even more information.

Safe people know how to give good advice at the right time. Some people desperately need advice, but they won't listen until they feel accepted. If we insist on telling them what to do when they don't want to hear it, we often alienate them even further. And sometimes the real reason we want so badly to give advice that will help fix the other person's problem is so that it won't bother *us*. (Ouch!) Be slow to give advice. Wait until the person feels safe. At that point he may ask for advice or you can ask for permission to give it: "Would you mind if I give you some advice?" If he says no, go back to square one!

The cardinal rule for relating to young people is this: Earn the right to be heard by listening carefully, understanding fully, and avoiding condemnation.

Getting Help

If you care about an adolescent, you need to know when it's time to get additional help. You've learned to be a safe person who displays warmth, shows empathy, listens, and gives good advice. But you need to be sensitive to a teenager who is in need of immediate help, looking for someone to intervene. This young person may be depressed, suicidal, or homicidal; he may struggle with addictions to food, alcohol, drugs, pornography, or something else. Talk to your pastoral staff to find the care that is appropriate. No matter what, don't give up hope. God will provide someone who can give the teenager you care about—and his whole family—the help that is needed.

Don't wait too long to seek help. It never hurts to talk to a pastor, counselor, or wise friend as soon as concerns surface. You might be able to help your teenage friend work through the problems before they reach a crisis.

If the young person is part of your family, pride may get in your way. Many of us don't want other people to know our families aren't quite as perfect as we'd like for others to believe. So we wait . . . and wait . . . hoping things will change. Take the initiative to get the input you need. You might find out that you simply have unrealistic expectations about adolescents and the solution is for you to lighten up! On the other hand, you may realize that it's time to take steps that will change the destructive direction of someone you love. Make the call. Take the time to get the help all of you need.

If you are a friend of a hurting teenager who has told you some things in confidence, you may find yourself in a big dilemma: Should you talk to your friend's parents or youth pastor and try to get help for her, or should you keep quiet and not break her trust? That's a hard one. My rule of thumb is this: If you have any questions about the need to get help for your friend, talk to your youth pastor or school counselor. Let that person take the initiative to talk to your friend and see what help is needed. If the parents need to be brought in, let the youth pastor or counselor make the call. You can tell your hurting friend that you needed some advice, so you talked to someone who can help . . . and who is trustworthy. You take some risk that your friend will get upset, but that risk is far better than letting your friend self-destruct.

I hope the insights in this book are helpful to you as you care for the most wonderful people in the world—young adults!

Reading More about Helping Teens

Bustanoby, Andre. *Being a Single Parent.* New York: Ballantine, 1987.

Campbell, Ross. *How to Really Love Your Teenager.* Colorado Springs, Colo.: Chariot Victor, 1993.

Carter, William Lee. *The Angry Teenager.* Nashville, Tenn.: Thomas Nelson, 1995.

Carter, William Lee. *Why Did You Do That?: Understand Why Your Family Members Act As They Do.* Wheaton, Ill.: Tyndale House, 1996.

Dobson, James. *Love Must Be Tough: New Hope for Families in Crisis.* Dallas, Tex.: Word, 1996.

Dobson, James. *Life on the Edge.* Dallas, Tex.: Word, 1995.

Ezzo, Gary, and Anne M. Ezzo. *Reaching the Heart of Your Teen: Basic Communication between Teen and Parent.* Sisters, Ore.: Multnomah, 1997.

McDowell, Josh, and Bob Hostetler. *Handbook on Counseling Youth.* Dallas, Tex.: Word, 1996.

McDowell, Josh, and Bob Hostetler. *Right from Wrong.* Dallas, Tex.: Word, 1994.

Parrott, Les III. *Helping the Struggling Adolescent.* Grand Rapids, Mich.: Zondervan, 1993.

About Al Denson

For over twelve years, Al Denson has been a leading light in music ministry as a singer and songwriter. Having performed for more than two million teenagers in youth rallies and festivals, Al has established a rapport with America's young people that is without equal.

In 1994 he won the Gospel Music Association Dove Award for Choral Collection Album of the Year: *Al Denson Presents the Youth Chorus Book, Volume II.* His CDs include *Be the One; Take Me to the Cross,* which has a companion devotional from Tyndale by the same title; and *Tabula Rasa.* Al also has a weekly teen television talk show, *Studio 828,* which airs on FamNet affiliate stations. Many times he has been the featured performer with Billy Graham, Franklin Graham, and Dawson McAllister. And twice he has hosted Youth for Christ's Congress on Youth Evangelism.

In early 1998 a series of enthusiastically received high school concerts helped Al recognize the Lord's leading down a new pathway. He now does as many as three high school assemblies a day, speaking and singing to around 4,500 teens each of those days. Making it clear that he is a Christian, Al invites the young people to an evening concert, where he is able to speak fully about his faith. The free evening shows average around 3,000 young people.

Al and his wife, Tracie, live in Dallas, Texas, where they attend Las Colinas Fellowship.

About Pat Springle

Al wrote this book with his good friend Pat Springle.

Pat is the vice president of Quantum Leap Productions, and he is president of Baxter Press. With a master of arts degree in counseling, he served as senior vice president of Rapha Treatment Centers for three years after being on staff eighteen years with Campus Crusade for Christ International.

Pat has authored or coauthored over twenty books, including *Trusting: Learning Who and How to Trust Again,* *Co-dependency: A Christian Perspective,* and *The Shepherd's Way: Rapha's Advanced Training for Lay Counselors.*

Pat and his wife, Joyce, live with their children, Catherine and Taylor, in Friendswood, Texas.

OPERATION CHRISTMAS CHILD

Operation Christmas Child is a project of Samaritan's Purse, an international Christian relief and evangelism organization. This unique project sends a message of hope to children in desperate situations around the world through gift-filled shoe boxes, relief aid, and Christian literature.

Operation Christmas Child provides an opportunity for individuals of all ages to be involved in a simple, hands-on missions project that reaches out to needy children while focusing on the true meaning of Christmas—Jesus Christ, God's greatest gift.

Every year thousands of churches, schools, and organizations around the world participate in Operation Christmas Child. Last year we collected over one million shoe boxes from across the United States, Canada, Europe, and Australia and distributed them to children in dozens of countries throughout Latin America, Eastern Europe, Africa, Asia, and the Middle East.

How to Fill a Shoe Box

Find an empty shoe box. You can wrap it—lid separately—if you would like, but wrapping is not required.

Determine whether your gift will be for a boy or girl and the age category: Infant, (2–4), (5–9), or (10–14). Place the appropriate boy/girl sticker from your brochure on the TOP of your box and mark the correct age category.

Fill your shoe box with a variety of gifts from the following categories:

- Small toys: stuffed animals, dolls, balls, cars, etc.
  (No toy guns, knives, or other war-related items, please)

- School supplies: pens, pencils/sharpener, crayons, coloring books, writing pads/paper, solar calculator

- Hygiene items: toothbrush, toothpaste, soap, comb/brush

- Other: T-shirts, socks, Bible-story picture books, sealed hard candy/gum *(No other food items, please)*
  Please do not include items that may easily break or leak.

You may enclose a note to the child and a photo of yourself or your family. *(If you include your name and address, the child who receives your box may write to you.)*

Enclose **$5** or more in the envelope from your brochure and place it in your shoe box to help cover shipping and other costs related to Operation Christmas Child. **(Checks are recommended rather than cash. If you or your family are filling more than one shoe box, you may make one combined donation in a single envelope and place it inside any one of your boxes.)** Place a rubber band around your shoe box and lid.

For shipping and collection information, or if you have any other questions, call 1-800-353-5949.